Sandie & Lee

Thanks so much for your
leadership of the Global 6K!

Praise for Michael Chitwood and
THE ABILITY TO ENDURE

"Heartbreaking. Encouraging. Passionate. Look out. This book may bring you to tears. It may inspire you to run a marathon or change the world. Michael Chitwood has that effect on people, and this book will show you why."

RICHARD STEARNS, president of World Vision U.S. and author of **Unfinished and The Hole in Our Gospel**

"Michael Chitwood is one of the first people I met when I showed up at my first Team World Vision meeting in 2010, scared out of my mind. And his face was one of the first I saw when I showed up to the TWV tent the morning of the marathon, still scared out of my mind. I knew he was a great coach, a passionate advocate for people in need, a serious runner. But I didn't know the heart of what brought him to running and to Team World Vision. This story was a gift to me, and a must-read for anyone who believes that healing sometimes comes in unexpected places."

SHAUNA NIEQUIST, author of **Bread & Wine and Savor,**
shaunaniequist.com

"Hold on tight. *The Ability to Endure* is compelling, challenging, and inspiring. It will take you to the deepest lows and highs of your own soul, yet not leave you there, compelling you to ask, "What difference can I make in my own life and that of others?" Ultimately answering the very human quest for our purpose in life, Michael's story and words hold honesty, vulnerability, truth, pain, and joy at the same time. Honestly, it has been such a long time since I've read such a serious yet refreshing book in the social good arena. *The Ability to Endure* is a kick to the soul, very much needed in our present world. You won't put it down. It's a must read."

PRINCESS KASUNE ZULU, founder of Fountain of Life non-profit organization and author of **Warrior Princess**

"I was reading *The Ability to Endure* when I was going through a particularly trying time in my running career. Michael's words encouraged me to endure my rough season every time I picked it up. His story inspires me to love deeply, hurt with life's losses, and then rise again. No matter where you are in your race of life, you will undoubtedly find inspiration in Michael's story and find the strength to endure through life's tough stretches."

RYAN HALL, two-time U.S. Olympic marathoner,
U.S. half-marathon record holder

"I had a dream—to win the Olympic Games. That dream became reality because I had a coach. Someone who taught me the right techniques to elevate my performance. Someone who saw my potential and helped me unlock it. Someone who showed me the light when things got dark. Someone who knew about going through struggle and coming out a stronger person. I have another dream—to be a great person. In that pursuit, Michael Chitwood has been one of my best coaches."

ASHTON EATON, world's greatest athlete, world record holder–
decathlon, U.S. Olympic gold medalist–decathlon

"A powerful story of loss, love, hope and inspiration. *The Ability to Endure* captures your heart from the very first page, rallies your inner strength, and teaches you how to thrive through life's greatest challenges."

JENNY HADFIELD, **Runner's World** columnist and author of
Marathoning for Mortals, jennyhadfield.com

"At the heart of this book is an invitation—to choose how you let your circumstances affect you and the call God has put on your life. Michael Chitwood shares how he has pushed past great pain and disappointment to continue to dream and live a life of immense influence. In doing so, he will inspire you to find what waits for you on the other side of the painful experiences in your life if you will trust God to lead you through it."

SARA HALL, two-time U.S. track and field world team member,
U.S. national cross country champion

"Hilarious. Devastating. Inspiring. Hopeful. These four words describe the journey you will take as you read *The Ability to Endure*. Complete with a unique mix of humor, pain, vision, and promise, Michael will inspire you for more. Every so often a book comes along that jolts you into a better version of yourself; that moment is right now."

JON PEACOCK, lead pastor, Mission Church, wearemission.com

"*The Ability to Endure* is a real story of putting faith into action and inspired me to do the same. The redemption and heartbreak in this story shows how being a positive force in the world after dealing with loss is no easy task but the rewards are lasting."

ALAN WEBB, American record holder in the mile, U.S. Olympian, professional triathlete

"Michael Chitwood's book is a moving read, shedding light on both pain and hope. He has courageously taken a route few dare take—of being vulnerable, sharing his pain and struggles. Through the book he shares how we can overcome the darkest of pains in our lives. Michael has inspired me and many people through his daring spirit, to dare the seemingly impossible. I never used to run until I met Michael and the Team World Vision guys who inspired me to try it. Today, a good number of my Kenyan colleagues also are running for charity. Of greatest impact to me was learning two things: remember the poor, and the body can do almost anything you put your mind to and train it to do."

JUSTUS KOECH, World Vision Kenya, Donor Liaison

"*The Ability to Endure* is proof that putting one foot in front of the other can make the world a better place for the less fortunate. Michael's transformation from a defensive lineman to ultrarunner with a mission to change the world will inspire thousands."

BART YASSO, Chief Running Officer, **Runner's World** magazine and author of **My Life On The Run**, BartYasso.com

"One does not forget meeting Michael Chitwood. Within five minutes he had convinced me to help hundreds of children in South Africa and run an ultramarathon. Which we did! Through that experience I learned Chitwood's incredible story, one that I tell frequently as a source of strength, inspiration, and hope. The losses Michael has experienced in his life have been so repetitive and crushing, it makes one shudder. Yet time and time again, he has gotten back up, stronger in spirit and resolve, leading and motivating others in his mission to help the poor. Read this book and it will change your life, just as Michael's friendship has changed mine."

LIEUTENANT COMMANDER ANDY BALDWIN, M.D, U.S. Navy physician, humanitarian, media personality, nine-time Ironman, and former star of ABC's "The Bachelor." drandybaldwin.com

"Michael's candid journey through success, loss, personal discovery, and faith moved me to my core. The words of his journey spoke to my soul, reminding me to cherish the simple joys in life and relish in the miracles that reveal themselves through faith."

LOPEZ LOMONG, two-time U.S. Olympian, 2012 Visa Humanitarian of the Year, and author of **Running for My Life: One Lost Boy's Journey from the Killing Fields of Sudan to the Olympic Games**

"Growing up in South Africa, I was wrecked by apartheid. I always wondered, what is my role in global poverty, in meeting the needs of the poor? Michael Chitwood was the one that unlocked this question and invited me to get in the game and live a better story! Michael is a leader, a true friend, and a man who'll give his very last breath to bring hope to people in poverty. This book is packed with true grit, blood, sweat, and tears, and a fight to change lives. I urge you, read it, and get ready to be called out for the sake of the least of these."

PAUL JANSEN VAN RENSBURG (JVR), pastor and director of section communities, Willow Creek Community Church

"Michael loves encouraging people to do something that really matters. In *The Ability to Endure*, we are invited into the story that fashioned him into a man who lives what he believes. This story is raw and honest, yet buoyant and full of hope. Michael has been my friend for almost a decade. We've been telling him to write a book all that time. Read it and you'll find out why."

DARREN WHITEHEAD, pastor, Church of the City, Nashville, TN, and author of **Rumors of God: Experience The Kind Of Life You've Only Heard About**

"As a seasoned runner (Team World Vision), pastor and friend of Michael Chitwood, I had high expectations regarding this book. However, I did not expect the level of motivation and encouragement I received. This compelling story is a narrative of God's grace, running through pain, suffering, and triumph. It helps us finish with hope. *The Ability to Endure* will inspire you to run your life on purpose!"

BOB BOUWER, Sr. Pastor, Faith Church, 1 Church – 8 locations

The Ability to Endure

THE ABILITY TO
ENDURE

MICHAEL CHITWOOD

Published by THE RUNMOTIONAL PROJECT.

Chitwood, Michael.
The Ability to Endure

ISBN: 978-1-4951-6515-3
eBook ISBN: 978-1-4951-6516-0

Printed in the United States of America

Cover design by Michael Forsberg
Cover photography by Kendra Stanley Mills
Interior design and layout by Weykyoi Victor Kore

First U.S. Edition 2015

Contents

Part One: Before the Loss

Part Two: Between One Loss and Another

Part Three: After

Dedication

To my family, which has had to endure more loss and pain than I could have imagined possible, and has found, through its faith, the ability to endure.

To my dad, who first showed me that we meet Jesus in the lives of the poor. To my mom, who raised me with an unconditional love that helped me catch a glimpse of the love God has for us. To my brother Dan, who was always my biggest encourager. To my brother David, who showed me how to love all people. To my nieces and nephews, who have had to face far too much pain at much too young an age. To my brothers' wives, Kim and Jamie, who have faced unbearable heartbreak. To my Kenyan family, Josphine, Justine, Shadrack, Japheth, Millicent, Astone, Elias, Jacqueline, and Maurine, who have shown me the heart of God.

To my wife, Dani, who has been my constant source of calm in the midst of life's storms, who has believed in me and supported me even in my craziest of dreams. To Cruz, who has shown me that despite life's darkest hours, the sun will rise again and hope is alive in this world.

And to all those who have faced unspeakable pain in this world and cried out to God. To all those whose faith has been crushed under the weight of pain, grief, and loss, I pray that even when God doesn't make life easier, somehow you find He will give you the ability to endure.

Foreword
by JOSH COX

The first time we ever spoke, we were on the phone for two hours. I shared my story and he shared his – they were different but the same. We had suffered loss, endured pain, and we wanted our lives to matter. We both had been to Africa, and had a passion for the poor and the marginalized, but Michael Chitwood was actually doing something about it, and I didn't know where to begin. His story and that phone call changed my life.

I was a professional distance runner, coming back from a two-year hiatus from the sport while I cared for my dad during his nine-month battle with cancer – and the subsequent aftermath when I questioned if running mattered at all. Did times, teams, records, and contracts have real meaning? The records were on loan, others would fill the podium and the money would come and go. What difference did it make? I've always been pretty introspective, but watching my dad — an NCAA champion wrestler, a man who made millions in business — wither away during the nine months from diagnosis to death, transformed me. That time put an old head on young shoulders, gave me a new lens on life, relationships, goals, the things I wanted to do, who I wanted to become, and it made me question the trajectory of my life.

Toward the end, my dad told me something over and over that I'll never shake: "I thought I'd have more time." His plans and dreams were left undone in his fifties. I didn't want to wait to make a difference; tomorrow wasn't promised, tomorrow was a lie. It gave me a sense of urgency and made me evaluate everything. I didn't want to spend my whole life climbing a ladder only to realize I had it propped against the wrong wall.

Eventually, I came to realize running wasn't trivial; it mattered because it was a gift that had been entrusted to me. My passion for running and passion for the poor wasn't trivial, either, our talents and passions never are.

I fell in love with Africa when I went to Kenya to train with Kenyan running royalty, Moses Tanui, a two-time Boston Marathon champion, a track world championship gold and silver medalist – he's a big deal, a Kenyan Michael Jordan, if you will. Each morning, Moses would drive us out to a training camp outside of Eldoret. The runners lived well, but my heart broke when I saw and experienced the poverty all around. I wanted to help but didn't know what to do – other than give kids bananas in the afternoon and empty my suitcase before I left.

When I returned home to San Diego, I couldn't get them out of my mind, the memories haunted me. I began educating myself. The more I read, the more I understood the issues: access to clean water would cut the child-mortality rate of kids dying before age five in half. Immunization, sanitation, education, basic nutrition – small things we take for granted, literally save lives. In this day and age, a child shouldn't die because of a lack of food, clean water, or a 30 cent immunization – I believed these to be inalienable truths, but believing something wasn't enough; never has been and never will be. Writing is cheap, talk is cheaper, and creeds without deeds are dead. Actions wail – words whisper. Doers change the world.

When Michael and I chatted on the phone that afternoon, we shared a common burden for the poor. But he had a real plan, a road map. His beliefs, intent, and ideas had moved from his head and heart to his hands. Michael was a doer, he had been moved to action and he was inviting me along for the journey. I wanted to be like him. I wasn't exactly sure what I would do. I didn't know how I could help, but I knew that I would finally be doing something. I would help the helpless, be a voice for the voiceless. My walk would finally back up my talk. I'd be an ambassador; I'd go see the work, I'd do the work, my running would have a real purpose. It wouldn't be just about winning races or making teams; it would be about saving lives and giving children a future, rewards that would outlast any medal or olive wreath.

I was galvanized as I listened to him. That day, he encouraged me with his story and motivated me with his words. But it has been his dedication to the dream and consistency throughout the years that has changed my life and countless others. Michael is a man who leads and inspires by example.

Through our years of friendship, I've been educated on social-justice issues, seen entire communities transformed by those who run races for a purpose, witnessed the impact and long-term benefits of clean water pipelines, wells, rain catchments, solar power, agriculture, education, nutrition, sanitation, and infrastructure. These are all amazing byproducts of him tolerating me and putting up with my nonsense. But what I treasure most is that he's shown me there's a purpose in our pain, nothing and no one is beyond repair, no task is too big if we have a faith that moves mountains, following our heart and pursuing our passions is never a mistake, and finding a way to use our talents and passions to serve others is the bedrock and cornerstone of true success — how we outlive our life and leave a lasting legacy.

Michael and his story have helped me hope more, dream more, believe more, and do more. Each time we journey to Africa, it's a reset button for my life. Each time we talk, he reminds me of what really matters. He has let me know, time and again, that I'm not alone in my pain and my struggles. He's let me know I have a friend. I love him for his authenticity and his willingness to share. I love him for who he is and who he wants to be. I love him for believing in me, even when I don't believe in myself.

I laughed and I cried on that first phone call with him many years ago. As you move through the pages that follow, prepare yourself for the same as you hear from my friend's heart and listen to his story. Like me, you will be inspired by his resolve and moved to action by his life.

Introduction

ENDURE: verb
1. *to hold out against; sustain without impairment or yielding; undergo*
2. *to continue to exist; last*
3. *to suffer patiently*

As human beings, we are able to endure far more than we would ever believe possible. Stories like Chariots of Fire and Unbroken capture the ability of human beings to push beyond what we believe are human limits. Like most people, I stand in awe at the harrowing feats people like Erik Liddell and Louis Zamperini were able to accomplish; the obstacles they were able to overcome in order to triumph. I've often wondered how I might respond under similar circumstances. Would I have the physical and mental resilience to endure like them if I were put to the test?

Most people who push the far reaches of their physical limits usually do so not by choice but as a result of the circumstances they're born into or fall into. Refugees who are forced to flee their homeland endure unlivable conditions for months or years on end. Children born into extreme poverty survive on meager meals so infrequent and lacking in nutrition that their tiny bodies cease to grow, yet still, they survive. For those of us who have never known the pangs of hunger, the fear of war, or thirst so strong we would drink disease-ridden water to stay alive, we will likely only ever catch a glimpse of our true limits. We will never have to fully realize just how much we can physically endure.

For most of my adult life, I've been pushing the limits of my own physical capacity, developing my body's ability to endure athletically over long distances. I didn't become an endurance athlete because I'm anything like Erik Liddle or Louis Zamperini. Originally, I became a long-distance athlete because I didn't want to be fat anymore. It started with a marathon, then an Ironman triathlon, then an ultramarathon, then a 100-mile run. With each increase in distance and physical challenge, I tested the limits of my body — and my mind — their ability to endure.

Much like our physical bodies, our soul also can endure more than we might imagine. While many of us are protected from the gravest of physical harms, none of us will escape some form of emotional pain in our lifetime. At some point each of us will face something that seems unbearable, and we will doubt our own ability to survive the pain, the loss, the heartache. We will question our ability to endure the circumstances we find ourselves in.

While you may never know fear that comes from not knowing where your next meal will come from, maybe you have experienced the helplessness of watching a loved one suffer from an incurable or debilitating disease, or perhaps your own body has fallen victim to such a fate. Perhaps the pain you have suffered has been the result of a broken marriage, an absent parent, the loss of a child, a struggle with infertility, or some other shattered dream. Maybe, like me, you have cried out to God, "I don't think I can take anymore!"

Pain is a certainty in this life. It is guaranteed to find us. At times it may feel like grief has sought us out. When we face this type of suffering, our instinct is to run from it. But no matter how we try, we simply cannot outrun it.

This book is about pain and loss and heartache. It's about being at the end of yourself — losing faith in anything and everything, and then finding hope in the strangest of places. Finding redemption where it seems least likely that God would ever show up. It's about how when you think all is lost, it isn't. How when it seems like there is no reason to take one more step forward, there is. It's about realizing our instinct to run when life gets tough. And it's about wanting God to make life easier, and instead he gives you the ability to endure.

Part One
Before the Loss

Part One: Before the Loss

African Sky

"How great is it that nobody need wait a single moment before starting to improve the world."

ANNE FRANK

My head lays heavy on the cheap, flattened pillow, and my feet hang off the end of the bed, which is a few inches too short for me. The lack of a fitted sheet on the thin mattress is a small distraction from the knowledge that there may be a spider the size of a small rodent somewhere behind the seatless toilet in the corner of the room.

The mosquito net tucked at the edges of the bed, now familiar to me, took some time to get used to and protects me from buzzing pests that carry malaria. The walls of this room are painted cinder block; the floor is concrete. I have a shower, but the hot water only works on occasion. Sometimes it gives me a small electric shock because of the outdated heater the water passes through just before coming out of the opening where a shower head should be. The electricity is turned off for the night because the gas for the generator is expensive, so I let the stars shine in through the windows that fortunately for me have screens on them.

The rain makes music on the corrugated tin roof, and I think of the child, Maurine, who sleeps just a few miles away with no such shelter. She sleeps on a dirt floor in a mud home with a thatch roof, and I wonder how she gets any rest when it rains.

Sleep isn't coming easy to me this night as my mind drifts over the events that have brought me this far. Not just to this place in the world, this remote village in the Great Rift Valley in Kenya, but to this place in my life. The undeserved advantages that I have been given; the unspeakable pain I have come to know personally, intimately. Sometimes I think I must be one of God's favorites to have been given such opportunities, such privilege.

But those thoughts are fleeting as I remember the pain that has brought me here, the loss that I have suffered, and the times I have wondered if God had forsaken me.

Tragedy can set in motion all sorts of events. It can drive you into deep despair; paralyze you, trapping you forever in the grief of a single moment. But it can also light a fire in you, wake you up, make you realize that you are not promised another year, another day, another breath. You have but one life, and it is yours to waste or live to the fullest.

The trajectory of my life has been greatly directed by a few events I never saw coming. Some have been moments of utter loss and pain; others have been invitations to walk through fear, and do something beyond myself.

Through these events, I have come to believe some things. First, there is more pain in this life for me than I could have ever imagined possible; second, my pain pales in comparison with the pain of others, and God expects me to do something to relieve their suffering; and third, almost every good thing that God has for us in this life lies just on the other side of fear.

On this night as sleep evades me I wonder, without the pain I have endured, the loss I have suffered, would I be here in my favorite place on earth, on the other side of my fear, underneath this African sky?

Wake-Up Call

"Never awake me when you have good news to announce, because with good news nothing presses; but when you have bad news, arouse me immediately, for then there is not an instant to be lost."

NAPOLEON BONAPARTE

It is rare that I go to bed before my wife, Dani, but it had been a long day at work and I hit the hay shortly after talking to my mom on the phone. She had called to tell me that Dad's surgery earlier that day had gone well. It was just a routine shoulder surgery, but Dad hated the hospital. It wasn't like him to feel so at peace in a hospital room. He had gone through several back surgeries, and being put under for surgery had always made him nervous. But he insisted Mom go home and get some rest. Other than a case of the hiccups, Dad was doing great, she said.

Dad occasionally got the hiccups for days at a time, keeping him from getting any sleep. The nurse planned to give him something to stop the hiccups before bedtime, Mom had told me.

Since she had gone back to teaching, Mom and Dad seemed to relate to one another in a way I had never seen before. Dad had become more thoughtful, especially in regard to supporting her work.

Mom had first become a teacher in the late 1960s during a teacher shortage and was able to teach without having finished college. When my oldest brother Dan was born, she quit teaching to stay at home with him, then David, then me. When I was in middle school, Dad convinced her she could go back to school and finish her degree so she could teach again. I was only thirteen at the time, but the thought of my mom sitting in a classroom with a bunch of college kids made me proud of her. I knew even then that she was afraid to go back to school, and it was only because of Dad's encouragement that she had the courage to try.

When she finally finished school, she struggled to find a teaching job. She applied to every school within two hours of our home. No one was hiring, but Dad wouldn't let her quit. He was in her corner the entire time, encouraging her. She finally found a teaching job in one of the best school districts in Michigan, just a few years before Dad retired.

The night of his surgery, she left the hospital reluctantly and only because she had a big Mother's Day tea planned for her first graders and their moms the next day. She left Dad's hospital room and headed home, but not before stopping at the nurses' station one more time to remind them to check in on him and telling them that sometimes a spoonful of peanut butter helped with the hiccups.

I was glad to hear his surgery had gone so well. Knowing how my dad hated the hospital, I felt bad that I had forgotten to call him that morning. How could I have forgotten to call? I told myself I'd call him in the morning. I was planning to head home that weekend to see him, and for Mother's Day. I was sure he would be excited to hear we were coming. His boys were his world and to have one of us fuss over him made him feel special.

Dad's childhood had been tough. Growing up with an abusive, alcoholic father, he appreciated our family far more than any of us ever understood. My dad never uttered a mean word to any of us, despite the fact that his own father had been cruel and had thrown more than verbal attacks at his wife and kids.

I remember falling asleep especially fast that night after my mom's call, too tired to even turn on the TV. Dani had fallen asleep on the couch in the living room, another rarity, which is why she was awakened first when the phone rang at about one o'clock in the morning. Asleep in our bedroom, the ringing phone woke me only halfway, until Dani rushed into the room.

"Michael, wake up. Wake up! Your mom is on the phone crying. Something happened to your dad!"

Part One: Before the Loss

Mutt

"I'm so mean, one time a rattlesnake bit me; and it died."

ARTHUR "MUTT" CHITWOOD

"Run, Byron! Run!"

His mom had called him Barney ever since he could remember. Whenever she called him Byron, it meant one of two things. Either he was in trouble, or his dad had been out drinking and had come home cussin' mad, and then they were both in trouble.

He didn't remember his dad any other way than the way he was now, mad and drunk most of the time. Barney's mom said he used to be different, nicer before the wars and before the accident. His dad had fought in the First and Second World Wars, and he wouldn't let you forget it. It was maybe the one thing he was most proud of, the only thing he had to be proud of. Both of Barney's older brothers, Gene and Doug, had fought in the Second World War. Gene actually lied about his age to get into the Army. He was just sixteen when he enlisted. They were all off to war when Barney was born. But it wasn't the wars that made his dad so angry all the time. It wasn't the wars that made him drink. It was the pain.

His name was Arthur, but everyone called him Mutt. He used to be a coal miner. He kept his mining helmet and head lamp on a desk in their sitting room, the kind of lamp that used oil to keep a flame lit so the miner could see where he going in the deep, black of the coal-mine shafts. Right after the war, when Barney was too young to remember, there was an accident at the mine where he was working.

They were nearly a mile down in the mineshaft just about to break for lunch when something went terribly wrong. The coal dust moved through the shaft in an unnatural way as if to let the miners know that something terrible was about to happen. They sensed it before they heard the snap of one of the support beams. It gave way and came down on Mutt hard, pinning him face down on the ground with four hundred pounds of rock weighing on the busted beam; the weight of the world holding him down. He couldn't move, couldn't breathe. They said it took six men four hours to dig him loose. Mutt broke his back. He spent weeks in the hospital and never fully recovered.

Barney's mom said that's when hate took hold of his dad. "Barney, don't ever become a hateful man like your father," she told him. "God has better plans for you. Big plans."

Mutt never talked about the wars, and only talked about the cave-in at the mine once in a while. But he talked about the pain in his back all the time. You could tell by the way he walked, a little bent to the side and sort of dragging one leg behind him, that it hurt bad, and you could tell by the anger in his voice and slur in his speech how much he'd had to drink. That's when things started to get worse, after he broke his back.

When he was little, Barney's mom would tell him to run to the neighbor's house any time she heard his dad coming home from the bar. "Run, Byron. Run," she'd whisper to him in a fearful voice that trembled and sounded like a quiet scream.

So he would run, out the back door of their house so his dad wouldn't see him leaving. Sometimes he'd run to the neighbor's house, sometimes down the street past his school to where his friends Jimmy and John lived, and sometimes all the way past the prison that was a few miles from his house. He used to run and hide out for hours, until long after the sun went down.

When he would come home, his mom would be in the kitchen crying quietly so she wouldn't disturb Mutt, who would usually be in their bedroom "sleeping." That's what she called it when he passed out drunk, the alcohol and cigarette smoke on his breath still hanging in the air. The bruises his hands left on her body didn't compare to the scars his words left on her soul. She would hug her son close and tell him she was all right, they would be all right.

That's what happened when Barney was little, before he really understood what happened to his mom every time she told him to run. Then one day, he stopped running. At ten, he decided he was not a little boy anymore. He would not let his mom take the punches his dad was handing out when he got home from drinking. He thought about the story his mom had told him about the day she found out she was pregnant with him.

Before that day, she had decided she had taken all she could handle from Mutt. She was planning to take her own life. The next time Mutt passed out drunk, she would put on her favorite dress and take a long walk through Canon City where they lived. She would climb onto the middle of the world's highest suspension bridge spanning Royal Gorge, say a final prayer asking God to forgive her for this last act on earth, and then she'd step off the edge to end her misery.

But something changed her mind. That very day she found out she was pregnant with Barney. She had told him at least a hundred times that he was the only reason she didn't jump off that bridge, that she knew God had a purpose for bringing him into her life.

"He has big plans for you, Barney," she'd tell him for as long as he could remember.

Whenever he walked past that bridge after school, he felt proud that his mom thought he was worth living for. In a strange way, her story made him feel like her protector, like he had kept her from dying, from jumping off that bridge.

He felt like her protector now too. He wasn't a little boy anymore. So when his mom told him to run that day, he didn't run. Instead, he stayed.

Mutt had hit Barney before. But the first time he stayed and told his dad to stop hitting his mom, he exploded.

"Do you think you're a man now?" he screamed at Barney. "What right do you have to tell me what to do or not to do? This is my house, and I'll do whatever I want, and I'll hit whoever I want."

Barney's dad towered over him, alcohol on his breath and fury in his gaze. The tears began to well up, but he held them back, kept them from running down his cheeks as he stared his father down. He was afraid, but he had decided he had to stop running.

He didn't remember much after the first blow. But he did remember being embarrassed to go to school the next day. The lies came easy to him when he needed them. For a long time, he had to give an explanation for every black eye or bruised arm. After a while, people just thought he was clumsy, that he had two left feet. At least they stopped asking all those questions.

He couldn't understand why all this was happening to him, to his mom. It didn't make any sense. Sometimes he would ask God how He could let his dad be so cruel and mean. It didn't seem like this was how things were supposed to be.

He promised himself that when he grew up, he'd never be like his dad.

My Dad

"My father gave me the greatest gift anyone could give another person, he believed in me."

JIM VALVANO

"…my hardships are nothing against the hardships that my father went through in order to get me to where I started."

BARTRAND HUBBARD

My dad never laid a hand on me or my brothers, Dan and David. He never so much as raised his voice to my mom. In all my life, I never saw him take a sip of alcohol. Dad was a cycle-breaker. And while he rarely talked about his own father, he was determined to make sure he would be nothing like him. In many ways he ran as far from his father as a man could run to make sure he was different.

I was ten or eleven before I could throw a ball better than my dad. The first time I realized this, we were in our front yard tossing a baseball back and forth. I noticed he didn't have any sort of throwing form. He just flung the ball toward me the way a four-or five-year-old might throw a wiffle ball. The ball got to me, it just wasn't pretty.

I felt embarrassed for him. I didn't want him to know his ten-year-old son could throw a ball better than him, and I certainly didn't want him to know I saw it too. What I didn't realize then was Dad had missed out on just about everything a father could teach his son, every good thing anyway.

I got over him not being able to throw a ball because he never missed any of my games and never criticized how I played, not once. He wasn't like my friends' dads, who criticized them all the time, pointing out every missed tackle, dropped ball or bad pass. My dad had a sort of blind optimism when it came to his boys.

When I was about fifteen, I realized that as much as I needed my dad's love, he needed mine even more. He lived for my brothers and me; we were his everything. He may not have shared much about his dad, but Mom shared enough for me to know I shouldn't be too disappointed that my grandfather died before I was born. I knew enough about him to know I wouldn't have enjoyed Mutt's company much, and to understand my dad was his complete opposite.

Even in the old pictures of my grandfather, there isn't the least bit of resemblance to my dad, the way there is such uncanny likeness between me and the black and white photo of my dad when he was a young school teacher, newly married to my mom. Take away his suit and tie and black-framed glasses, and it's easy for anyone to see the resemblance. At six feet, four inches, I am a full head taller than my dad, but when standing next to him no one would need to ask if I was his son.

Even though my dad couldn't teach me how to throw a ball, he taught me plenty of other things, good things.

He taught me how to paint houses and paid me well to paint with him during the summers he had off as an elementary school principal. And when he had to stop painting, he taught me to run a painting business for myself.

He taught me to build things with wood, like tree forts and tables, and how to hang drywall and roof houses and fix a broken toilet.

He taught me to use a camera, and to sketch a blueprint for a deck. He taught me to use a saw, a hammer, and every other tool in his workshop in our basement.

He taught me that when your dad tells you you're awesome at everything you try to do, although you get a little embarrassed that he seems to say these things even when other people are around, you start to believe him, to believe you can do anything.

In the 16 years I played football, second grade through college, my dad only missed two games, both for family weddings. Both times he was upset our cousins had decided to get married during football season. He showed up for every talent show, recital, and parent-teacher conference. He was there for every important moment in my life. He taught me that sometimes just showing up and being present is the best way to say "I love you," but sometimes you still need to say the words.

My dad kept his promise. He was nothing like his father.

The Long Road Home

"I pray because I'm helpless."

C.S. LEWIS

I was only half awake when I took the phone from Dani, but I woke up fast at the sound of my mom's sobbing. She was on the phone and in a complete panic. The hospital had just called. Dad's breathing had stopped and as a result, so did his heart. They used the paddles on him, jump-starting his heart. They had him breathing again with assistance, but he had slipped into a coma.

The words didn't even seem real as she was saying them to me. Maybe she'd had a nightmare. She was in such frenzy and was barely making sense through her crying and screaming. It was clear she was having trouble even breathing.

No one was answering the phone at my brother David's house, which was just a few minutes from Mom and Dad's in Michigan, while my brother Dan and I lived more than four hours away in Illinois. I told Mom to give me a little time to get ahold of Dan and David on the phone. If I could reach David, he could come and take her to the hospital. But no one was answering at either house.

Dani packed a bag for us as I rushed to my brother Dan's house. At two o'clock in the morning, his entire family was in bed sound asleep. Banging on his bedroom window not only woke him, it almost gave him a heart attack. Dan has nightmares and doesn't wake easily. When he finally realized it was me, he let me in the front door and listened as I told him what would be only the beginning of the bad news.

It didn't take long for him to pack up his wife, Kim, and their four kids, while I went back home to pack with Dani for this unexpected road trip. We met in Dan's driveway and the eight of us headed out in two cars on the longest drive of our lives. We called Mom and David a few times an hour on our cell phones hoping for some good news, but none came. Only waiting and driving. David and Mom were at the hospital, and a helplessness I'd never felt before overwhelmed me as we made the long trek to Grand Rapids, crying, praying, and hoping.

Childish Dreams

"There is nothing like a dream to create the future."
VICTOR HUGO, LES MISÉRABLES

I felt two arms bear hug me from behind as my feet left the ground. He was nearly a head taller than me, and was holding me off the ground squeezing the breath right out of my lungs. I couldn't breathe and was struggling to find a way to defend myself against this giant. So I did what any six-year-old would do. I swung my right foot as far forward as I could, then swung it backwards kicking him right where it counts. He dropped me immediately.

That's my first memory of my lifelong best friend, Timmy Nelson.

We were in Mrs. Barber's first-grade class. It must have been raining outside or snowing bad, because we had indoor recess. That's when the weather is too bad outside and the teacher has to let twenty-five crazy first graders run around like wild animals in the classroom.

Two things happened that year when I was just six that I wouldn't fully appreciate until decades later. First, I met my best friend. Second, I fell in love with Africa.

I vaguely remember Mrs. Barber coming to class on Show and Tell Day with souvenirs and artifacts from her summer trip to Africa. I remember her looking a little silly as a short, gray-haired, older white lady dressed in an authentic African dress and a head wrap.

At our church, missionaries would come to share stories about what they were doing in the remote parts of the world, places like Mrs. Barber had gone. I remember thinking how cool it would be to be like one of them. But I also remember thinking most of them seemed pretty strange. They looked like Mrs. Barber but less cool.

I remember seeing images on television of hungry kids so unbelievably thin, their bodies little more than skeletons with skin, and their eyes begging for help. It made my heart stand still. Images of the famine in Ethiopia and celebrities singing "We Are the World." I remember how people would make jokes about how skinny Ethiopians were. Some people seemed to think these jokes were funny. I never did. Even as a kid, my heart broke for these children.

These are my earliest memories of Africa, of kids a world away, kids who didn't have a chance. Kids like me, only different.

I dreamed about what it would be like to go to those places and help those children.

Kiara

> *"Give justice to the weak and the fatherless; maintain the right of the afflicted and the destitute."*
>
> PSALM 82:3

David Letterman donated a big white gazebo to the city of Kankakee, Illinois, because the American Traveler's Atlas had just rated it the worst place in America to live. Kankakee is where I took my first job after college.

In my family, there were two basic career options. You could be a preacher or a teacher. I chose the latter. I had always hated school, so I figured maybe I could make school a better experience for kids like me, kids who had learned to hate school. Turns out, they were the ones who would teach me.

It was during my first year teaching fifth grade at King Middle Grade School in Kankakee that I had my first real, personal experiences with poverty.

Kiara was ten years old. Her hair was so matted it nearly formed into dreadlocks. Her thick Coke-bottle eyeglasses were scratched and broken, and her winter coat had a distinct smell. I couldn't place the odor, but I'd smell it coming down the second floor hallway as she walked slowly to our classroom, head down, unconcerned about being late for the start of the school day. She had a look in her eyes I had never seen before, one of utter disinterest. Not anger. Not sadness, although she did seem sad most of the time. I later came to recognize it as the look of hopelessness.

Every day Kiara fell asleep in class; every day she came to school that is. But I could tell from the little bit of schoolwork she did complete, she was extremely bright. She was possibly the smartest kid in my class but was pulling straight F's. Something wasn't adding up.

I decided to make a home visit to see why she was so tired all the time and struggled to get any homework done. It was early fall and the sun was down by the time I headed to the address our school secretary had written on a Post-it note. With a higher per capita murder rate than Chicago, there were a lot of areas in Kankakee most people wouldn't want to go by themselves during the day, let alone at night. I had done a few home visits already that year and thought I had seen the worst there was to see. I was wrong. I wasn't prepared at all for what happened next.

Had I written down the address wrong? This didn't seem like a home, or even an apartment building. I walked through the doorway in the back alley that shared the building number with the piece of paper in my hand. I entered the building to find people slumped on the floor in the hallway. Nearly everyone in this place had the same look in their eyes as Kiara had every day at school. A woman behind a small table passing for a desk asked who I was and who I was there to see. She made me sign into a registry like I was visiting someone in the hospital.

"What is this place?" I wondered. She walked me down the hall and up a poorly lit stairway in the back. The smell of Kiara's jacket filled this hallway, this entire building. Halfway down the hall we arrived at a door and the woman simply said, "This is her room." She knocked on the door and walked away.

The door opened and Kiara's mom stood in the doorway, surprised to see me. The room was about the size of my own bedroom.

But this wasn't Kiara's room. This was the room Kiara shared with her mother and five siblings. Seven people lived in this one room.

This was the first time I had seen the inside of a homeless shelter, the first time I had a reason to. It was just down the street from the school and until that moment, I didn't even know it was there. It was no wonder this little girl rarely got her work done and slept all day in class. Kiara was the first homeless person I had ever met.

I kept asking myself, "What has she done to deserve this?" She was just a kid. She didn't have a choice in any of the things that were so drastically impacting the trajectory of her young life. The cards were stacked against her, and the dealer had no intentions of shuffling the deck. She would have to play with the cards she'd been dealt. It just wasn't fair.

That first year of teaching, I got trampled by those ten-year-olds. For all my good intentions, I was ill-prepared to help the kids that were in my charge. They came from homes that were nothing like the one I grew up in. Of the sixty students in my class during my three years as a teacher, only two lived with both parents, and many lived with neither. Instead they lived with aunties and uncles, grannies and grandpas, or with foster families.

So many things about our lives are out of our control. Where we are born, the color of our skin, the family we are born into, the schools we go to when we are young. So many of the accomplishments in my life I had attributed to my own hard work seemed completely unrealistic and out of reach for the kids in my class. They had none of the advantages in life I had always taken for granted. I had two parents, both with college degrees, who loved me and told me so often. I went to a school that graduated almost 100 percent of its students, with most of them going on to college. I grew up with coaches who taught me to be a leader, friends who made doing good in school the norm, and countless other blessings that would take me years to recognize for what they were — advantages.

Some days when I got home from teaching, it felt like I had been run over by a semi or had just played in a football game with a 350-pound offensive tackle smacking me around for four quarters. I was exhausted and my body ached. To see kids living in such heartbreaking situations was beating me up, breaking me down. It all seemed so unfair. The obstacles these kids faced seemed nearly insurmountable.

Poverty had never been a part of my world. I lived far from it, safely protected in my comfortable bubble in the suburbs of Grand Rapids. I didn't know poor people, and so I didn't spend much time thinking about them. But now, poverty had a face, the face of a ten-year-old-girl named Kiara, a girl without a real chance at life. Her pain was all I could think about.

I'll Do Anything

"A man of faith does not bargain or stipulate with God."

MAHATMA GANDHI

Every feeling imaginable overtook me on that drive to the hospital. Being strong for Mom on the phone just hours ago was difficult. Fighting back the tears was my job. But now, alone in the car with my wife, Dani, they began to roll. It felt like waves of fear crashing over me. One minute I was being pulled out to sea by a riptide, sure I was about to drown, the next I'd catch a glimpse of the shore and realize it was still there. That I hadn't drowned yet, that there was still hope.

Horror eclipsed hope as I imagined the nightmare this life would be without my father. I struggled to push away the fear, telling myself there was no reason to think this way, to assume the worst. So I drove into the dark night, eyes forward, fighting back the tears for long periods of time until they filled my eyes and streaked my face, and then finally erupted into uncontrollable sobs.

Dani put her hand on my shoulder and tried to encourage me, telling me it was going to be all right; Dad would be OK.

The ringing phone that woke me just hours earlier now seemed years in the past, and I could barely remember how the car I was driving had come to make its way home to Grand Rapids. I only remember stopping once at a rest stop to talk to Dan and let the kids use the restroom.

The sun was barely rising when we pulled into the parking lot of the hospital. As we rushed into the building, it felt like time was at a standstill. So much had changed in the hours of that night. I had already begun bartering with God, making deals with Him. If only He'd give us a miracle, I'd give up anything or everything. I'd be a better person. Tragedy can bring out the salesman in most of us. We try to sell God anything we think He'll buy. Anything we think He might want. Anything to get what we want.

Mwen Grangou

"When I was hungry, you gave me something to eat."
JESUS CHRIST

My dad was an elementary school teacher and principal for thirty-five years. When I graduated from college, I took a long-term substitute teaching job at his school for five weeks and got to see him in a new light. He was an incredible principal, a real leader. The kids stood up straight when he walked through the halls, and the teachers all loved him.

He had started bringing teams of educators from the U.S. to help train teachers in developing countries, most of whom never had the opportunity to attend college. In this work, my dad had finally found what he was put on this earth to do. He was about to retire and give all his time to this new teacher training ministry. Two years after my five-week subbing stint at his school, Dad had planned to take a team of teachers to Haiti. He invited my mom, Dani, and me to come with him. So I went.

This was ten years before the Jan. 12, 2010, earthquake that wreaked havoc on Haiti. But it was already the poorest country in the western hemisphere. My dad prepared me pretty well, or so I thought, for the heartbreaking poverty we would witness. Stepping out of the Port-Au-Prince airport, I could almost feel the presence of poverty in the air, an aura. It's a distinct feeling you come to recognize over time. It's an overwhelming experience to see people who have no opportunities to work, no access to food, education, or even safe water to drink. That feeling isn't so different from one impoverished place to another. The air in Nairobi, Addis Ababa, or the Townships in Johannesburg all have it, a shared quality that's hard to put a finger on. But you never forget the first time you experience it.

The abject poverty invades your senses, and it either breaks your heart and draws you in, or drives you to turn your head and ignore its existence.

"Mwen grangou! Mwen grangou!" cried small, glassy-eyed children, barefoot and in tattered clothes, as they ran alongside our SUV as we drove through Port-Au-Prince. "I'm hungry! I'm hungry!"

Tears filled my eyes and streamed down my cheeks. My heart was beating faster and there was a pit in my stomach. I ached for these kids. As I was crying, a few of the other people in the truck giggled nervously and took pictures.

I saw my dad in the front seat, his eyes filled with tears. He didn't speak. I could see how his heart had been broken by this place. I could see why he wanted me to come here with him.

We were here to train teachers. There were seven American teachers, including me, who were supposed to be leading workshops on lesson planning, science, math, geography, classroom discipline, and my subject, creative writing. I had just finished my second year of teaching, so I felt a little unsure how much I would have to offer.

Approximately two hundred Haitian teachers showed up for the training. Some had walked for four or five days to be at the sessions we would hold in a small village a six-hour drive from Port-Au-Prince.

Among the fifty teachers that filed into the cinder block room with a corrugated tin roof that served as the classroom where I would teach my seminar the first day, there were two extremely young teachers. These two boys were fifteen and sixteen years old. They were teachers. At the time, in that part of Haiti, you only had to have completed one grade level above the grade you were teaching. Someone with an eighth-grade education could teach seventh grade.

These two boys taught sixth grade in the morning and attended high school in the afternoon. None of the Haitian teachers had attended college. All of them had class sizes of fifty or more students at a time. The books they had to teach from, if they had any books at all, were written in French, because there were no textbooks printed in the national language of Haiti — Haitian Creole — which has only been a written language since the 1980s.

On that first day, I experienced a helplessness I'd never felt before but have felt a thousand times since. My eyes were only beginning to be opened to the realities and challenges faced by these teachers on a daily basis. It left me with a broken heart that has yet to mend.

During lunch that day, all of the teachers filed into a larger building on the school grounds. This building was also built of cinder blocks with a corrugated tin roof and spaces for windows with metal bars in the openings. We were served a meal of rice and beans with a little bit of chicken. Most Haitians, we learned, ate once a day, and it was typically just rice and beans. Even the teachers who were sitting in that room with us would likely only eat meat once or twice a year. They were planning to serve it to us every day.

As we began to eat our fill, the open spaces that passed for windows in the cinder block walls began to fill with eyes peering through as tiny brown hands clutched the rusty iron bars that formed a crosshatch that would have been the window pane, had there been any glass. While we ate generous portions of rice and beans and chicken, children watched us through the open window spaces with hunger in their eyes. A few times the community leaders shooed the kids away, threatening to whip them with thin branches pulled from trees if they continued to make the visitors feel uncomfortable.

The American teachers, the same ones who had giggled nervously on the day of our arrival, begged the local teachers to let us give the leftovers to the kids. There was so much food surely we could share what was left. But the local teachers knew this was not a simple problem. Poverty is complex, and so are sustainable solutions.

We didn't understand the problems we were creating. There would not be enough food to feed every child, so who would determine which kids got fed and which ones didn't? And what about tomorrow and the next day and every day after we were gone?

No matter how hard it was for us to understand, they would not give the extra food to the kids. My stomach turned. I cried. Felt helpless. Felt their helplessness.

Dad had done an incredible job preparing us for this trip — my mom, Dani, the other teachers, and me. But honestly, there is no way to really understand until you look a hungry child in the eyes and feel their despair. Dad was there to help me through it, help me understand my responsibility.

It was on that trip that I rediscovered my childhood dream about wanting to help people in other countries who lack the basic necessities of life.

I came back from Haiti with an application for a job as a teacher at a school in Port-Au-Prince. Dani and I talked about the possibility of moving to Haiti after we got married so I could teach there. But fear won out.

So many people close to me told us that living in a developing country during our first year of marriage would not be a good idea. Not a safe plan. So I caved in to the fear. I listened to the naysayers instead of God. I took a job with Campus Life working with high school students in Champaign, Illinois, a great but fairly safe job. Any dreams of helping the poor would need to wait.

That trip to Haiti helped me understand what was going on in my dad's heart, why these trips were all he could talk about. I got to see him become the man God created him to be. It was like the thirty-five years he spent as a teacher and principal had all been training for this, for helping the poorest people in the world.

My dad may not have been able to teach me how to throw a baseball, shoot a free throw, or make a tackle, but he taught me the important stuff, like what compassion looks like. As he traveled to some of the most broken places in the world, I watched his heart break for people living in abject poverty and saw him do everything in his power to relieve their suffering.

Desperate

"Even when I call out or cry for help, he shuts out my prayer."

LAMENTATIONS 3:8

Completely exhausted from the drive through the dark hours of the night and the energy spent forcing back tears and bartering with God, my recollection of the next few days is a bit foggy. The memories are more like the way I think of my grade-school days as a kid. Specific events are clear, but the moments that connect them are missing or clouded. Like how I remember the color and texture of the rug I slept on at naptime in kindergarten. How I remember indoor recess and snow days. And my best friend Timmy, attacking me in first grade and kicking him where it counts, and our teacher sharing about her trip to Africa.

That's how I remember those days after that phone call. Those days that followed our drive home through the night. Those days in the hospital by my dad's bedside, praying for a miracle. At times it still feels like I'm trapped in those moments when our faith was strong and hope so sure. I remember calling my mother-in-law and her praying with me on the phone. I remember being at my parent's home and trying to sleep through one night but instead just lying on the floor hoping for a miracle.

For three days after the phone call, I spent most of my waking hours with my mom and my brothers at my dad's bedside as the doctors prepared us for what they said was the inevitable, that eventually they would likely need to disconnect the machines that were making his blood pump; that were making his lungs breathe in and breathe out. They had jump-started his heart, kept his lungs and heart working with machines, but he remained in a coma. They told us he was gone, that his brain showed no activity at all, that my dad wasn't "in there" anymore, that there was no hope.

But they wouldn't have the last word, these doctors. They were wrong. We would show them they were wrong. We believe in a God of miracles. We believe in a God that can heal people — make sick people well, lame people walk, raise people from the dead. I knew that God would show up in that room with us. We prayed, and I believed wholeheartedly that at any moment he would sit up in his bed, healed. I had been taught to pray for miracles. I had been taught that God could heal. I believed He would.

My brothers, my mom, and I stood together in the hospital room. My wife, Dani, and Kim and Jamie, Dan and David's wives, couldn't handle being with us. They were too afraid of what might happen. Maybe they couldn't stand to watch us go through this.

The heart-rate monitor beeped every few seconds, and the distance between the beeps grew longer. Still I knew, beyond any doubt, that God would heal him. We were praying at his bedside, and I knew God would heal my dad. It couldn't end this way. God wouldn't let it. We held on to hope for a miracle.

My entire life I'd been taught God always answers our prayers. I had never prayed so earnestly as I had those three days before Mother's Day 2001. Going on little sleep, I wandered the halls of the hospital, made phone calls to friends and family from a pay phone to give updates and ask for prayers, took uncomfortable naps on waiting-room chairs, and sat at my dad's bedside as he lay motionless. With any twitch of a muscle or fluttering eyelid, I convinced myself there was hope.

My faith wavered but never gave way. Too many things still had to be done. Dad had just started this incredible work with teachers in the poorest countries in the world. Certainly God had bigger things in store. Dani and I didn't have any children yet. We would need him there to be Grandpa, to help me learn to be a dad. He was too young. He had too much left to do. He was too important to me to lose him now. I needed him.

The steady beeping sounds coming from the machines measuring my dad's breathing and heart rate was what held me together, reassured me that hope was still alive, that dad was still alive. Beep. Wait. Wait. Wait.

Beep.

And so that beeping sound became my comfort.

We held hands as we prayed. I couldn't tell what was going through my mom's mind or my brothers'. Did they still believe? Had their faith been shaken?

Beep. Wait. Wait. Wait. Wait.

Beep.

Never have I relied on hope like I did that day, desperate for a change in what was happening to my dad, my family, my life. Desperate. A word I was truly unfamiliar with until that Mother's Day. Most of life had been handed to me: an amazing family, great friends, great schools, incredible opportunities. There had been no real opportunity in my life to know what desperation was. But standing in a family circle, hands locked to one another, crying out to God in desperation, I found myself utterly helpless and fully dependent on God to move this mountain.

Beep.

As the beeping sound coming from the machines slowed, fear

rose up in my soul. My heart was screaming to God to move in this moment, to do what I knew He could do — what He needed to do — to change this outcome. Make this moment different from the one it seemed set on becoming.

Beep.

The distance between beeping sounds grew greater and the beeping slowed until, at last, it become a steady tone. Only then did it become clear to me that my dad was not going to sit up in that bed.

I learned that day that if God does indeed always answer prayers then sometimes He answers with silence, indifference, or a simple and resounding "no." It became apparent the God I thought I knew wasn't who I thought He was at all.

My heart was broken. My dreams were lost. My faith was shattered.

Alone

"For no one is abandoned by the Lord forever. Though He brings grief, He also shows compassion because of the greatness of His unfailing love."

LAMENTATIONS 3:31-32

She was alone. We were standing in the family waiting room at the hospital. My whole family was there, my brothers, our wives, aunts, uncles, friends, cousins, all there with my mom. But on the other side of the room, where people get the worst news imaginable, stood a woman all by herself.

I would guess she must have been a few years older than my mom, maybe even a decade. She had just received the same news about her husband — he was gone. I have no idea how he died. Cancer maybe? A heart attack? I watched the doctor and could tell by his body language and hers what he was telling her. She stood there by herself for a few minutes, trying to process what she had been told. She looked lost, a deer in headlights. I should have walked across the room and tried to comfort her, but I was in no shape to try such a thing. I couldn't move. I was paralyzed with grief of my own. After some time, she left.

That woman has invaded my thoughts a thousand times since that day. Why was she alone? No one should be alone when they get that kind of news. I can't imagine walking through the pain and loss with no one by my side.

In the months and years that followed the loss of my dad, I've had my wife, Dani. My brother Dan had his wife, Kim. My brother David had his wife, Jamie. My mom had … no one. I don't mean to say we didn't try to be there for her. She had us, her sons. Her parents. Her brothers and sisters. She had more people than the woman in the hospital appeared to have. But we didn't face each day with the same loneliness she did. She had lost the person who had walked with her through every pain and loss she had experienced in her adult life. For all practical purposes, she was alone.

Part Two

Between One Loss and Another

Part Two: Between One Loss and Another

White Castle

"Mothers hold their children's hands for a short while, but their hearts forever."

UNKNOWN

It was one of my favorite days with my dad. Almost exactly a year before he died, I got to spend an entire day with him, just me and my pop. It was early spring and Dani and I were getting married that summer. She had invited my mom and my soon-to-be mother-in-law to go shopping for wedding dresses. My dad came to Chicago with my mom so he and I could spend the day together while the women shopped.

We sat at a White Castle restaurant a mile from Dani's mom's house in Homewood, Illinois. It was a place he and I had never eaten at together because, sadly, we didn't have any White Castles where I grew up in Grand Rapids. We sat there for hours talking, and Dad opened up to me about things he had never told me, or possibly anyone. About how he wished he could tell my mom more often how much he loved her, and how he trusted her more with disciplining us when we were kids than he trusted himself because he never wanted to hurt us the way his dad had hurt him. He talked about how proud of me he was. But the one thing I remember most about that day was my dad talking about his mom.

We had been to visit my Grandma Chitwood just a few times in my life because we lived in Grand Rapids and she still lived in Canon City, Colorado, where Dad grew up. When I was in sixth

White Castle   69

grade, my dad told us we would be going to get Grandma so she could come live with us. Her health was deteriorating, and it was up to him to take care of her.

Dad built a small bed frame for the back of our Dodge Caravan, and we drove more than twenty hours to Canon City to pick her up. My brother David later told me that he first learned what compassion looked like watching Dad's heart break for his own mother as he brought her home in the back of that minivan.

I was too young to fully understand what my dad was going through, watching his mom slowly become weaker and weaker, as he switched roles with her to play the parent and once again become her protector.

My memories of Grandma Chitwood living with us aren't clear. I remember that it felt awkward, like a stranger was living in our house, an old lady stranger who walked around in a burgundy bathrobe most of the time and made me feel a little embarrassed to have friends over to the house. I remember how my mom cried a lot during the year Grandma lived with us, and how my dad cried when they finally moved her into a nursing home.

I remember her house in Canon City, and I remember her being at our house for Christmas. But what I remember most about my grandma is something my dad told me about her the day we spent talking at White Castle, something I wouldn't really understand until the day he died. "Michael, I've never gotten over losing your grandma," he said.

This confused me. My grandma died when I was eleven. I was just a kid, and while I loved her, I didn't really know her. I couldn't really remember Dad talking much about her since she died, but then again he was a pretty quiet guy. It hadn't occurred to me the hurt he felt at the loss of his mother. Of course, the obvious just now dawning on me, my grandma was my dad's mother. For some reason this fact had never really connected with me. And I dreaded the kind of loss he described that day, the kind of loss I might never get over.

When I was a kid, I always had a deep fear of losing my mom. From the time I was between ten and fifteen, I had three close friends who lost their moms, one to cancer, another to a car accident, another to emphysema. So in my worst dreams, it was always my mom whom I lost. I never dreamed I could lose Dad. Maybe I thought he was too strong, indestructible.

Losing Dad changed everything. I had a new reality, one that didn't include him.

Everything I had ever imagined doing or becoming or experiencing would now be different. Going forward I would need to dream new dreams, ones that didn't include him. I needed to adapt to my new reality.

My dad would miss so many things, so many moments. I found myself worrying a lot about things that were years, even decades away. Things like whether I would be able to do a good job describing my dad to my kids one day. The kids I wouldn't have for years to come. The kids my dad would never meet.

Would there be any way they could ever know a man they had never met? What if I forgot the sound of his voice, or couldn't remember his laugh?

And what about the dreams we had together? After that trip to Haiti, we had planned to go on more trips together, to help train teachers in developing countries all over the world.

All the dreams of what my future would be like always included my dad in some way. Even the dreams in which he wasn't at the center, he was always there on the periphery, present. Now I had to dream about a new future, one that didn't include him.

This new reality took some time to sink in. On far too many occasions, I would dial his number, hoping for some advice about something, or just calling to talk, and not realize until the second or third ring of the phone that he wasn't going to be on the other end to pick it up. He would never be on the other end again.

And if Dad would never be there to pick up the phone and talk to me, then who would walk me through filling out my taxes, or signing a mortgage on a house, or lighting the pilot on our furnace? Who would encourage me to chase my dreams? Who would tell me I was awesome at everything I tried, and that I could be anything I wanted? Who would have that kind of blind optimism about the possibilities for my life?

The house I grew up in was empty in a way that is hard to describe. It was still filled with the same things that had always been there, but the feel of it all was different, less than it was before. Dad wasn't there. He never would be again. The feel of being in the house that he had designed himself and helped build with his own hands, without him being there, clouded my thoughts. I noticed things about the house in a new way. I realized that even the house would go on moving, changing without Dad sitting in his recliner falling asleep watching TV and answering us when we'd ask, "Dad, are you sleeping?" by opening his eyes a little and saying, "I'm just resting my eyes."

As all of these new realities sank in, another one hit me even harder: Losing my dad would not be the last time I would experience grief like this in my lifetime. It would be the first of many more losses. I suddenly understood with jarring clarity that the longer I live on this earth, the more inevitable it is that I will feel pain like this again. I was living in the *after* of losing my dad, but living in the *before* of losing other people I love. I was barely surviving the pain of this loss. I wasn't sure I could handle something like this again but was certain I would have no say in the matter.

Part Two: Between One Loss and Another

The Second Life-Changing Phone Call

"The God of the Scriptures is irrepressibly communal, hopelessly familial and His whispers are still ours to hear."

BILL HYBELS

It was almost exactly two years after my dad passed away that I got another phone call that would change my life. It was an ordinary Saturday afternoon in early April, and I was wasting the day on the couch watching television. Dani was in the other room because, as still happens from time to time, we wanted to watch different shows. The phone rang, and when I went to answer it, she asked me to close the bedroom door where she was watching her show because I have a habit of talking too loud on the phone. Well, to be honest, I have a habit of talking too loud all the time, whether I'm on the phone or not. Dani could tell from the first seconds that this would be one of those long, loud phone calls with an old friend. It was Mark Smith.

Mark and I met in second grade, and we didn't hit it off at first. He went to our "rival school," Collins Elementary, but we had both joined the Forest Hills Youth Instructional Football League. Mark was on the red team; I was on blue. That year, we practiced in full pads for two months but only played one game at the end of the season. After that we played football together on the same team for the next ten years. During those years, Mark became one of my best friends, along with Timmy.

After our eighth-grade football season Mark, Timmy, and I

started walking up to the high school every day when school let out to lift weights with the football team and coaches. We would spend three days a week every week for the next five years together in that weight room.

Getting big became our job, and we got good at it. In eighth grade I was five feet, eight inches tall and weighed 135 pounds. By the time I graduated high school, I was six-four and 235. In four years I had grown a foot and gained 100 pounds. Playing defensive end for a college football team meant I had to get even bigger, so I did. I ate everything in sight, but I could never seem to break 250.

After college, Dani and I got married and I kept up my football eating regimen but stopped the workouts altogether. Within a few years I was up to 265. From time to time I would commit to losing weight but couldn't seem to get any results. I even tried the "Ab Shocker," that belt that attaches electrodes to your stomach to electrocute you into shape. In case you're wondering, it doesn't work. "Maybe I'm just always going to be a big guy," I would tell myself.

Mark played a couple of years of college ball too, at Albion College in Michigan. But, after his football days were over, he went from being a big linebacker at six-three, 220 pounds to a lean 185. He started running, biking, and hiking. It never dawned on me that Mark's weight loss was a direct result of the new sports he had picked up and the fact he had given up fast food almost entirely.

Mark had called to tell me he and his wife, Tamera, were planning to run the Chicago Marathon that October. It was only April, but he wanted to let me know so that we could plan to spend some time hanging out. I lived a couple of hours south of Chicago, and he wanted me to come up and watch them run. It didn't even dawn on Mark to ask his big chubby friend to run it with him. Why would it?

I didn't realize it then, but that conversation with Mark would change my life.

I felt something move deep inside me when he said he was running the marathon. It was something like a voice whispering to my spirit two words: "Do this."

I had no doubt I was supposed to run the marathon with Mark.

When I hung up the phone I walked into the other room and told Dani I was going to run the Chicago Marathon. Thankfully, she didn't laugh me out of the room.

Instead she simply said with utter confidence, "You can do this."

I was scared out of my mind. It was awesome!

Part Two: Between One Loss and Another

Almost Quitting

"Never, never, never give up."

WINSTON CHURCHILL

"If Oprah could do it, surely I can," I thought to myself as I decided to test the water with this whole running thing. Though I had never even run a 5K, I had to believe that if she was able to run a marathon, then I should be able to pull it off. I had no idea what the training would entail or how hard it might be.

For the first few weeks after signing up for the Chicago Marathon, I ran on the treadmill until I could run a slow two miles. It then occurred to me that our gym was two miles from our house, so I set out on my first real outdoor run since running 100-yard sprints for college football. Within three blocks, my heart was racing. Halfway there, I could barely breathe. With three blocks to go, I had to walk the rest of the way. I couldn't even run two miles, and I had just signed up to run a marathon! What was I thinking?

I wasn't very good at it, but I kept running. Within a month, I was running three miles three times a week. I was getting excited because now I was beginning to believe I could do this. When I started my goal was this: train for the marathon, and finish it in the time allowed. I figured if training for and running in a marathon didn't get me in shape, then nothing would.

It took a while for me to tell Mark about my plan to join him and Tamera in the marathon. I wanted to train up to six miles before telling him just to be sure I would be able to do it. Once I could run six miles, I let him in on my plan. He was excited and put his full confidence in me.

I'm a big mouth. After I told Mark about my plans, I began telling everyone. They weren't all as supportive as Mark. Some made jokes, some encouraged me and some outright told me I would fail.

One friend told me, "Michael, it's not that I think you can't do it. I just don't think you will."

After telling everyone I knew I was going to run a marathon, after putting up with the jokes and negative comments, the amazement, and 'atta boys, the worst happened.

I went for my longest run ever, a seven-miler, on a trail through the woods in Mahomet, Illinois. I loved this trail because there were markers to indicate every half-mile. My enthusiasm grew as I counted mile markers toward what would be my farthest turnaround point yet. The weather was perfect for a run; the sun shone through the trees, and I felt amazing. Like a runner.

Then, just as I was coming up on the 3.5-mile marker, the turnaround point for seven miles, I felt a sharp pain in my left knee. At first, I thought maybe it was no big deal. I stopped for a minute to walk it off. Then I tried to start running again. It was excruciating. It felt like someone was stabbing me with a knife right on the side of my knee. I walked a few steps, no pain. I'd try to run again STAB! STAB! STAB! I let out a few screams. Screams of anger, hurt, fear, frustration.

"This can't be happening!"

I could walk without pain. But each time I tried to run, it was like a knife stabbing me in the side of my knee letting me know that running back to the parking lot where I had started this, what was supposed to be my longest run ever, was not an option. As I hobbled all the way back to my car, I began to enter the depths of self-doubt. My eyes filled with tears.

What if this pain in my knee won't go away?
What if I'm just not cut out for this?
What if I can't do it?

The negativity began to swallow me up. I started to panic. I had already told everyone I knew that I planned on running in the marathon. I couldn't stand the thought of facing those who didn't think I would actually do it. Maybe they were right. Maybe I wouldn't do it. Maybe I couldn't.

The next day at work I told my friend, Ron, what had happened with my knee. He was one of the few people who consistently encouraged me. He knew just what to do. "Come with me," he said.

Twenty minutes later we pulled into Hatcher's Auto, a used-car lot. When I walked into his office, the owner sat behind his desk, bright white hair, skin that was tanned from countless hours in the sun, and a pearly white veneer smile.

"Hi, I'm Hatch," he said in a gravelly voice that sounded like he must have spent at least a good part of his life smoking.

Behind him, the wall was covered with framed marathon medals, Ironman medals, bib numbers from races, and pictures that told stories of the miles he'd spent, the blisters he'd suffered, the bragging rights he'd earned — more than thirty marathons, a few Ironman triathlons, and countless other races. And Hatch hadn't even started running until his mid-forties. When he first told his friends he had signed up to run his first marathon, they laughed at him.

Hatch told me, in his raspy upbeat voice, "You can do this." Next he asked, "Are those your running shoes? Where'd you get those?" He had a stern and confused look on his face.

They were, in fact, my running shoes. I was pretty proud of them. They were the coolest looking shoes I'd ever owned. I had gone out and bought the coolest looking pair of Nike's I could find, the problem was they weren't actually running shoes. It was obvious from Hatch's tone that something about my beautiful new Nike running shoes was all wrong.

Ron brought me to see Hatch because he knew I was close to giving up on running the marathon, and he knew I needed to follow through on this dream. He figured Hatch could encourage me. He was right.

Hatch told me the pain in my knee was very common for someone who was not used to running long distances. I.T. band syndrome he called it (iliotibial band syndrome). I needed to go to a real running store and get fitted for the right shoes. If I treated my injury correctly, he assured me, it would not be a long-term obstacle. Hatch's encouragement put a boost of confidence back where my painful run had left a hole. I had been so discouraged I almost quit. Almost.

Butterflies

"Keep away from people who belittle your ambitions. Small people always do that, but the really great make you feel that you, too, can become great."

MARK TWAIN

Every Friday night, I would lie in bed with butterflies in my stomach, nervous about the next morning's long run. How would I do it? It was a new first every week as each Saturday I did a run that was longer than I had ever done before. Running was new to me, and I was making improvements every few weeks. I could run a certain distance faster, or I would run a longer distance than I had ever done before.

I had no idea how to train for a marathon. I had found an eighteen-week marathon training program online and stretched it out over thirty weeks without adding a single run. This meant I was only running about half as much as I should have been. Not a good idea. But at least I had the right shoes, thanks to Hatch.

Training for the marathon was hard. Each day when it was time to go for my run, I literally had to make myself go. There were so many days the only reason I went at all was because I knew on race day Mark would be ready. He would definitely be more prepared than me because he had a head start by a few years on this whole running thing. So when I just didn't want to go, I went anyway.

When I began doing runs of more than nine miles, I had to slow down my pace, a lot. Some of my friends would comment on how slow I was after having seen me out on a run.

They'd say, "I thought you were training to run a marathon?" "I am," I'd reply.

"Then why were you out walking the other day when I saw you." "I wasn't. I was running."

"Oh. It *looked* like you were *walking*."

Ouch. That hurt.

None of them was a runner. In fact, I have never had a marathoner tell me anything like "you can't do it" or "you're so slow." Despite the naysayers and pessimists, I kept going on my runs, and they slowly got easier, but not much faster.

While running was getting easier little by little, I wasn't noticing much change in the way I looked. I wasn't even sure if I had lost any weight, so we bought a scale.

With no idea what to expect, I stepped on the scale for the first time. When I started the training two months earlier, my weight had been somewhere around 245 pounds. To my surprise, I had lost 20, but it didn't really show. At least I couldn't tell. But I told myself I would finish this, so I kept training.

That was the benefit of having committed to running a race that would require six months of training. It forced me to keep running even when I was discouraged with how slow the change was happening. A long race like a marathon requires training consistently over a long period of time. When I got discouraged about my progress, or lack thereof, I still had a goal I was working toward. I was a work in progress.

Losing weight was no longer the sole purpose of my efforts, but I was learning to enjoy the journey itself, even if I still kind of hated running. Not every time I ran brought moments of peace, but many of them did.

Through the Fog

"The Lord is close to the brokenhearted, and He rescues those who are crushed in spirit."

PSALM 34:18

It felt like a fog was slowly lifting. A small sense of clarity coming back to me. A feeling of normalcy, like nothing had happened. Like I was me again. As if my whole world had not been taken from me.

Then, without warning, I'd feel as though I had been slammed to the ground.

Blindsided. Brokenness would come over me heavy and dark, and quickly I would be reminded my heart was still broken. Tears would fill my eyes. My faith was still shattered. The moments of peace out on my runs were real, but they were fleeting.

It was April 2003, almost two years since losing my dad. Two years since my life and everything I knew to be true about it was changed. The decision to run a marathon had really been about losing weight, not about talking to God. Not about healing my wounds. Just me trying not to be fat. That's why I had decided to run 26.2 miles at the Chicago Marathon despite the fact I had never even run a 5K.

Now, this was before iPods drowned out the thoughts of most runners and Garmin GPS watches beeped at the mile marks. Afraid of being bored during what would be — due to my extreme slowness — a lot of long hours alone on the road, I bought myself an AM/FM radio and headphones to run with. I got a $10 Timex watch to time my runs. To figure out the distance of my route, I would drive it in my car, mark it off, and write the mile marks on a piece of paper: Prospect and Windsor Road (2 miles, turnaround for 4); Savoy 16 Movie Theatre (4 miles, turnaround for 8). I'd carry that piece of paper in my pocket when I ran so I would know how far I had gone. I'd use my $10 watch and the math skills I had gained during my years as a fifth grade teacher to estimate my pace. Twelve minutes per mile. That was my goal. If I could just hold that pace on all of my runs, I could finish the marathon in the required time an hour before they closed the course.

Looking back, I can't believe I even tried running with that radio. It was huge! It had a big antenna on it, like the one on my dad's old metallic blue station wagon with the far-back bench seat that faced the rear window. It looked like a blue version of the old school cell phone that Zack Morris had on "Saved by the Bell." I could never get that stupid radio to work right either. It wouldn't get any stations to come in clearly. Just static.

I felt maybe God was telling me to listen to a different station. I was like, "All right, God. I'll try the Christian station, if I must," knowing full-well I didn't care much for Christian music. Still, nothing but static.

The stupid thing wouldn't work. Maybe God really was trying to tell me something. Something like, "Chitwood, you look like an idiot trying to run with headphones and that massive sound machine that doesn't even work." I know I felt like an idiot. What did people think when they saw me, this big chubby dude running down the street, so slow it could barely be called running, big blue radio hooked to the waistband of my baggy sweatpants or tucked in the pocket of my hooded sweatshirt, out of breath?

I tried hard to look like a runner. I would even do that silly bouncing thing runners do at red lights to make it look like we are disappointed the light turned red just before we get there, knowing all the while we intentionally slowed our pace as we approached the intersection to ensure a bit of rest because, as usual, we went out too fast for the first mile of our long run.

After a time, I decided to give up that big, blue AM/FM radio. I decided maybe God was telling me something more. Something besides, "Chitwood, you look like an idiot." Something more like, "Hey, kid, I'm here. Are you listening? I'm speaking to you, and I need you to listen. I have some things to tell you."

Since that night two years earlier when the beeping machines keeping my dad alive stopped beeping, I hadn't felt much like talking to God. And when I did, what did I get? Just static. My dad's death proved that God wasn't who I thought He was. I'm not sure if I had been ignoring Him or if He just wasn't speaking to me, or maybe He was just giving me some time to cool off.

"All right, God, if that's You, I'll try to listen. I'll give You my time on the road. This time that's just supposed to be about not being fat. This running thing that scares me to death. This precious time, the only time in my life when my mind isn't racing so fast it hurts. The only time I'm able to, for a moment, forget about what happened. Forget how You hurt me. Forget the day my heart was broken. When my dreams were lost, and my faith shattered."

That summer I did all of my training runs without that giant blue radio. No music to run to. Just me, God, and the road. It felt like He was invading my space after having been gone a while. Stealing my only moments and places where the fog seemed to lift a little, if only for a few fleeting minutes. Where my heart felt something other than pain. It was out on the road on those runs training for my first 26.2-mile race that my soul began to heal. Running became my therapy.

On the Road

"Not that I am (I think) in much danger of ceasing to believe in God. The real danger is of coming to believe such dreadful things about Him. The conclusion I dread is not 'So there's no God after all,' but 'So this is what God's really like. Deceive yourself no longer."

C.S. LEWIS, A GRIEF OBSERVED

God had failed me. He wasn't who I thought He was. In that hospital room that Mother's Day when the machine that made the beeping sound slowed to a single steady tone, He had shown me His true colors. The veil had been lifted, the mask removed, and the revelation was more than disturbing. It was heartbreaking.

All my faith had been placed either in a fraud or an adversary. Either God couldn't save my dad, which meant He didn't have the power I believed Him to possess, or He chose not to, in which case He did not have the love for me which I believed Him to have.

It's an awful feeling, abandonment.

That first year of running, training for my first marathon, doing those first long runs, I found moments of escape from the pain and loss. Running offered a welcome distraction.

But something else happened on my runs, something more than distraction. Once in a while. Maybe because I wasn't listening to music. Maybe because there were so many things to think about, yet nothing to hold my attention. Maybe because of the sheer amount of time I was out on the road alone, because I was running so slowly that my friends thought I was walking. Maybe because I was ready to hear God, He began talking to me. And from time to time, on those runs, I began to listen.

The conversation wasn't always friendly. I had some things to say, some frustrations I needed to get off my chest.

How could You do this to me? To my family? To Mom? I thought You loved me. I thought You wanted good things for me. I never thought You'd hurt me like this. You aren't who I thought You were. I'm not sure if I want to know You anymore.

Sometimes I yelled at God. It seemed to me He could take it. It seemed to me He had it coming. It seemed to me He was listening, patiently. Even in the times when I didn't want God around, I knew I needed Him.

And then, there were moments on those runs when I felt something different. Something new. Something I didn't know I could feel. I felt safe. Not the kind of safe where you believe nothing bad can happen. I knew better than that. Hell on earth can be unleashed in a moment. In the blink of an eye. With one phone call in the middle of the night, your faith can be shattered.

I felt the kind of safe you feel when you're a little kid and you fall off your bike, and your dad picks you up and says, "You're okay, son. It's going to be all right. Now, you're going to need to get back on that bike. You can do it. I'm here if you fall again."

At times it would seem like three steps forward, two steps back. And sometimes it was, with training and in my conversations with God. But, slowly, I was gaining ground.

I Can't Breathe

"The world breaks everyone and afterward many are stronger in the broken places."

ERNEST HEMINGWAY

One day, my dad and I were standing at the end of our driveway talking by the cement mailbox. Our driveway was curved in an unplanned sort of way. My dad had told me many times how the contractors had curved it for some reason, even though it was supposed to be straight. I knew it was our driveway because of the white and gray brick mailbox, the one some neighbor kids had blown up with a few M-80s when I was a kid. Our neighbor had seen some kids messing around late one night by our mailbox. He was chasing them when the explosion went off. No one got hurt, but I remember being mad that some kids had blown up our mailbox.

The mailbox I was now standing next to years later. The mailbox that made me sure the driveway I was standing in was the one in front of my house. The house I grew up in. That's where I was standing talking to my dad.

I don't remember much about the conversation I was having with my dad that day. Well, I don't remember my half of the conversation anyway. My dad just kept saying, "It's all right. I'm all right." Over and over he said those words. "It's all right. I'm all right." I couldn't figure out why he kept saying it. Over and over. I'm not sure how long we talked. It felt like we were there for some time, but it's hard to tell exactly how long. That's all I remember him saying though, "It's all right. I'm all right."

Suddenly I realized, I couldn't breathe. I was suffocating. Like something was on top of me. Sitting on my chest. Crushing me. Keeping me from breathing. I could tell something wasn't right.

I remember thinking as I was standing in our driveway talking to my dad that something was off. Was it the color of the shutters on our house? Whose car was that in the driveway? Maybe it was the clouds. Maybe they were moving too fast, or too slowly. I knew something was different. This wasn't real.

It felt like I was trapped deep underwater. I could see the surface, but I couldn't get my head out, couldn't breathe. I was going to drown if I didn't find a way to get a breath. I was disoriented. I couldn't figure out what was happening. Was Dad still talking? I felt like he was, but I couldn't tell for sure.

The next thing I remember is screaming. Sobbing and screaming. In my bed. I realized now I was in my bed, back in this life, the life where my dad was gone. The one where I couldn't stand at the end of our driveway and talk to him anymore and hear him say that he's all right. That it's all right.

Those first few years after losing Dad were filled with nights like that one. I would wake up screaming, sobbing, barely able to breathe. Like someone or something was sitting on my chest. Like my heart, my soul, had just been ripped from my body. And Dani would lay there with me and whisper, "I'm here. You're okay. I'm here," as she held me and put her arms around me, one hand rubbing my back, the other on my face holding me close to her.

No one can prepare you for that kind of pain. That kind of hurt. That kind of loss. Before losing Dad, the worst heartbreak I had faced was breaking up with a girl. Not making the ninth grade basketball team. Failing a class. Almost getting fired from my first teaching job right out of college. None of these even came close. Before losing Dad, I didn't know what pain was.

Dani got me through. It must have been hard for her. We'd been married less than a year when it happened. This wasn't the guy she had married. This grown man, lying next to her sobbing like a child. Gasping for breath. Punching the walls. Screaming at God. This was definitely not the guy she had married. I don't know how she did it. I would hear her words, "I'm here; you're okay, I'm here," later. From God. When I was ready to listen.

It was only two years later when I would have to take everything she taught me about loving someone through that kind of pain and hurt and loss, and give it back to her. Her dad died almost exactly two years and six months after mine.

When I was a kid, if I wasn't getting my way, I would say, "It's not fair!" And my parents would tell me lightheartedly, "Michael, life's not fair."

After losing Dad I thought to myself so many times, "This isn't fair." And then, one day I said it out loud to my mom.

She gently reminded me of others who have truly experienced the unfairness of this life. "You know what isn't fair? What's not fair is kids who die because they don't have enough food to eat. What's not fair is children whose parents can't even afford to keep them, so they send them off to live on the streets. What's not fair is a pregnant woman in Sierra Leone having her unborn baby cut from her womb because two rebel soldiers want to bet on the gender of her child. That's what's not fair."

My mom had been to Haiti several times with my dad, including the time I went with them. She had seen his pictures and heard about the horrors he had witnessed in some of the most broken places in the world. As brokenhearted as she was, she was still able to remind me that others' suffering was great too.

Sometimes I still find myself face-to-face with my dad. Usually I recognize right away that something isn't right. That something is off. That I'm not really there with him, that he's gone. But now, when I realize what's happening, I do my best to stay in that dream. Because when I wake up, I sometimes forget what he looked like. What he sounded like. I forget how incredible it was to hear him laugh until he cried, usually at something he had said. Sometimes I forget that even though I lost my dad when I was twenty-five, that's twenty-five years longer than some kids have a dad. I forget I meant the world to him. That he loved me more than himself. I forget how lucky I was to have a dad who never criticized me. Never put me down. Never hit me the way his dad hit him. Because I know that when I'm awake, I forget.

Sometimes, I just want to stay there in that dream and talk with him a little while longer.

28,713

"The miracle isn't that I finished. The miracle is that I had the courage to start."

JOHN BINGHAM

By the time race day came, October 10, 2003, I had spent six months training and was down to 224 pounds, 21 pounds lighter than when I began, and 40 lighter than my heaviest. I could definitely tell a difference. Running was easier. I felt better. The change was slow, but there was definitely a change happening. Not just with my fitness, but deep inside me. All that training was over, and it was time to put my body to the test.

On race weekend, I asked Mark if he would run a race with me the next year. Before I even toed the starting line, I realized this race had changed my life. Little did I know just how big a change it would be.

The energy of the start line was so much like the nerves I felt on the football field waiting for kickoff. It was electric. Had everyone there just been through what I had? Had their lives been changed through these rare encounters with God out on the roads? There seemed to be a strange, shared experience that remained unspoken between me and some 35,000 other people waiting for the starting gun.

Mark had trained to run nine-minute miles. I had trained to run twelve-minute miles. We had not discussed a race strategy. I felt great running with Mark and his wife, Tamera (who was six months pregnant with their first kiddo), and we were clocking ten minute miles. "Wow!" I thought, "I am so much faster than I thought I was." At one point we came up on a guy running with a prosthetic leg. As we passed him, I was so inspired and offered some encouragement. "Come on buddy, you can do this!" I felt great right up until mile twelve. Out of nowhere the pain in my knee came back. The pain I hadn't felt since visiting Hatch at his car dealership and getting fitted for new shoes. The pain that felt like a knife stabbing me.

I started too fast and had to walk the better part of the second half. I would stop every half mile or so and stretch. I felt more physical pain than I had ever felt in my life. Around mile twenty, I heard someone yell to me, "Come on buddy, you can do this!" It was the same guy I had encouraged earlier, the guy with one leg. Mark stayed with me the entire time even though he could have easily finished over an hour ahead of me. I barely finished that race. But I finished.

Official time: 5 hours, 24 minutes, 37 seconds. I finished 28,713 out of 32,395 runners.

I felt like a champion.

I wished my dad were there.

Brothers

"What strange creatures brothers are!"

JANE AUSTEN

My parents told me that when I was born, my brothers Dan and David went door-to-door in our neighborhood proudly proclaiming they had a new little brother.

From the moment each of us was born, my dad began documenting our lives, in photos and on film. He was always behind a camera. In one reel-to-reel episode, he captured a scene with me at two years old; Dan and David were seven and nine respectively. I'm sitting on our lawn wearing plaid bib overalls with an unknowing smile on my face when my brothers enter the scene. Dan hands me the end of a garden hose. Meanwhile you can see David in the background holding a kink in the hose to make me think that the water is turned off. Somehow Dan convinces me to put the end of the hose in my mouth. What did I know; I was two? Just then David lets the water run full force through the hose. The hose shoots out of my mouth, but not before nearly filling my lungs and sending me into a full-on crying fit.

My brothers then rush over to comfort me, expressing their "sympathy" and trying to get me to stop crying. All the while the camera is still rolling. My dad tries to hold the camera steady, feeling a little conflicted as he continues to film, trying to decide whether it's better to intervene or to have a record of how much "fun" I used to have with my big brothers.

My brothers were best buds and worst enemies, and they couldn't have been more different. Dan was your typical first child. Type A personality, successful in everything he tried, but always because he was willing to work as hard as it took. David was a different story. Although he was two years younger than Dan, by the time he was five they were the same size. A lot of things came easy to David. He could ride a bike at four and dribble a basketball at five. When Dan learned to do something, David learned it too, despite the age gap.

The pictures of the two of them when they were young make it seem like they were always together, inseparable. My favorite picture is of the two of them at seven and nine, dressed as cowboys, standing back-to-back, pistols drawn. Best friends. But by the time they reached high school, their differences became increasingly apparent.

Dan was a firstborn all the way. He put his all into everything he did and always seemed to outperform his God-given talent. He got a college football scholarship as a linebacker even though he was only five-ten and barely 200 pounds.

Then when he sat the bench as a freshman he went to his coach and said, "Coach, I want to be a starter. Push me as hard as it takes, and I promise I will never ask you to back off."

Two years later he was not only a starter but a team captain. If you told Dan what it took to get something done, he would do it. Dan was a rule keeper.

In many ways, David had become the typical middle child, rebellious even if in mostly innocent ways. He steered clear of alcohol and drugs, but he had a Mohawk and earrings, and he got tattoos in high school. David stood six-three and weighed more than 300 pounds. He was the captain of the football team, but he didn't have to work all that hard for it. He was a natural athlete from a young age. He was big, but faster and more agile than anyone would guess by looking at him. Because things came easily to him, David never seemed to appreciate his natural ability.

David had a remarkable way with people, all people. He always seemed to know everybody, and they all loved him. He could see people for who they were, below the surface.

Bad luck seemed to follow David. I'm not saying he didn't make his own mistakes, that he didn't bear any responsibility for the circumstances he found himself in. Just that he seemed to get the worst of it more often than most. If ten kids were cheating on a test in school, he'd be the one to get caught. He seemed cursed by Murphy's Law. If something could go wrong, it probably would for him. David was a rule breaker.

I'd like to think I got the best parts of each of them, but I'm sure I got some of the bad stuff too. I was fortunate to have two heroes, both so remarkable in their own ways, and so different from one another. From Dan, I saw how hard work paid off. I learned determination to work against the grain, to beat the odds, and I learned discipline. From David, I learned to see all people the same, to be a friend to the friendless, to care more about what's inside a person than what's on the outside.

As a kid, my brothers were my heroes. But they were distant heroes. Five and seven years older than me, we didn't hang out much. It wasn't until I was in college that I started to get close to my brothers.

When I was home on summer break during college, David and I shared the basement at our parents' house. We worked together painting houses and spent a lot of time together. It was during those years we became good friends. He shared his friends with me. I got to see how they all came to him when something bad happened. He was their rock. Everyone he knew was touched by his compassionate heart.

Dan and I got close when I followed in his footsteps and played football at Olivet Nazarene University. He lived just a few miles from my dorm and worked at Campus Life, a youth program for high school students, so I started volunteering with him. It was during those years we became close friends. He shared his ministry with me. We played basketball, and tutored kids who came from tough home lives. The "at-risk" kids he worked with knew he was the one person they could count on.

As my brothers became two of my best friends, they slowly drifted apart from each other. After my dad died, the gap between them grew wider. I often felt like I was the connection point, the hub of the wheel, struggling to keep us all connected. As the unspoken distance between my brothers increased, I felt stuck in the middle. They were still my heroes.

Just One Drink

"Wine hath drowned more men than the sea."

THOMAS FULLER

"I was hooked after one drink," my brother David told me. I was seventeen, and he was twenty-two the first time he admitted he had a drinking problem. I was the only person he would tell for another ten years.

After high school, David passed on several offers to play college football to stay in Grand Rapids, close to his girlfriend. A few months later, she broke his heart. The next fall, he decided to join our older brother Dan at Olivet Nazarene University to play football, but his credits didn't transfer from Grand Rapids Community College, and he was ineligible to play.

Too much free time, a broken heart, and the wrong crowd turned out to be a dangerous mix. David told me the first drink he ever had was at Olivet, a private Christian school with a dry campus. He once told me his goal that year was to watch 1,000 movies in one school year. I don't think he came close to that goal, but he spent enough time not going to class that he lost his financial aid and had to move back home.

He moved into the basement, and I moved into the empty room next to his in the basement. He put a bed in the room where our shared drum set was and never minded when my grunge band had practice. We started to become close friends that summer.

The following summer, David had a terrible accident. He and

some of his friends were jumping of a cliff into a river using a rope swing. When it was his turn, his foot wasn't completely secured in the loop at the bottom. He was about 300 pounds at the time, the rope was wet, and he lost his grip and slipped off the rope swing. He fell thirty feet straight down the cliff, landing on a rock and shattering his ankle.

It took five or six of his friends to carry him back up to the car, and his injury required total reconstructive surgery to repair his ankle. For six months, he lay in bed in our parents' basement, which left him in a dark place, literally and figuratively. The pain from that fall would be something he would have to deal with the rest of his life.

The surgeon wanted to fuse his ankle, a medical procedure that would meld one bone to another, rendering the joint immovable. The doc said this would likely give him a better shot at walking normally and definitely would reduce his pain. But there was a three percent chance of infection, which, if it occurred would result in amputation.

David couldn't get over his fear of that three percent, so he opted not to let them fuse his ankle. For the rest of his life, he would walk with a limp and endure severe pain. His battle with weight went from bad to worse. During the six months of recovery from the ankle surgery, he put on close to 100 pounds. His broken ankle kept him a prisoner in the basement and pushed him into a deep depression, and alcohol was his only escape.

Alcohol and depression stole David's spirit, his personality, his self-worth, and his hope. He was one of the funniest guys you could meet. He had a laugh that was contagious, and he made friends easily. He clearly had a gift for making people feel comfortable, cared about.

David had more friends than anyone I knew, all sorts of friends. I can picture standing in line with my family to ride the Gemini roller coaster at Cedar Point amusement park. The sign at the entrance read 45 minutes from this point, but David saw it differently. To him it read, 45 minutes to make friends with as many people near you in line as possible.

He could make friends with anyone. He didn't have a "type of people." He had this unique ability to see the good in people, or at least to accept them with their flaws, to see everyone on a level playing field. From wealthy businessmen, doctors, lawyers and the like, to drug dealers, burned-out hippies, and homeless guys on the street.

In high school David signed up for adaptive P.E. It was a program in which kids helped special needs students. David helped several students through this program, but the guy he had the biggest impact on was a six-four, 260-pound kid named Drew. A developmental disability and paranoid schizophrenia made him a big target for other kids. In eighth grade, he was getting teased by some kids and lost his temper. He beat up one kid so badly that the guy was hospitalized. Drew was expelled and that's how he found himself at Forest Hills Northern High School in freshman P.E. with David as his adaptive P.E. helper.

David did more than help him in gym class. He became Drew's first real friend, the first person his age to ever treat him like one of the guys. Drew played on the football team, went to concerts with David and was at our home all the time.

David never viewed people as being better or worse than him. He had compassion for hurting people that was so much like my dad's. It's the thing I have always admired most about David.

While I'm sure he wasn't the only student who did a good job befriending the special needs students he helped, I'm willing to bet he's the only one who was still close friends with one of them twenty years later. Drew would go camping all the time with David, and his wife and kids. Thirty years later, Drew would still say David was his best friend.

It's true David had started drinking at college when my dad was still alive, but it didn't get really bad until we lost Dad. He just could not find a way to deal with the pain. While I knew from a young age that my dad needed my love even more than I needed his, the same was not true for David. My dad was his defender, his champion, his encourager.

I sometimes think it was a good thing David's drinking didn't get bad until after Dad died because I'm not sure Dad could have handled watching his son become so much like my dad's dad, Mutt. But then I think that if Dad hadn't died, maybe he could have helped David get through it, beat it. Or at least he would have been there to help Mom deal with David's drinking.

The toughest part of losing Dad was how it changed everything about our family. I don't think we realized how much Mom relied on Dad until he was gone. And this reliance was no more apparent than it was when it came to David and his drinking. We didn't grow up around alcohol. It was never in our house, and no one in my entire extended family drank alcohol at all. Not even socially. Now here she was, a widow dealing with an alcoholic son.

Our dad had worked so hard to break the cycle of alcoholism in our family, to not be like his dad. So when David started struggling with drinking, it must have broken his heart. I'm not exactly sure how it made him feel. We never spoke of it. We pretended it wasn't happening. David tried his best to hide his drinking, and we let him for years. We knew he had a problem, but we had no idea how to talk about it, so we just didn't.

One summer, when I was home from college on summer break and painting houses with David, I finally asked him, "David, do you think you have a drinking problem?" "Probably," he told me plainly, if maybe a little nervously.

We hadn't talked even one time about his drinking since I was seventeen, the day he told me he was hooked after one drink. We all just avoided the topic, so I wasn't expecting such honesty. People with drinking problems don't usually own up to it like that. Maybe I caught him off-guard with the directness of such a question in the middle of an ordinary day and otherwise meaningless conversation.

The only problem was, I had no idea what to do with this information. No idea what to tell him. This was the second time my brother told me he had a drinking problem. I am pretty sure I was still the only person he had ever admitted this to. I had no idea how to help him. And so I ran from the problem.

Part Two: Between One Loss and Another

Stuck

"Oh love, look at you now. You've got yourself stuck in a moment, and you can't get out of it."

U2

The death of a father can rock a family to its core. For some families, it's small, ridiculous fights over who gets what stuff, what to do with the house, or the surfacing of old wounds that were never resolved, words left unsaid, wounds left untreated that shake everyone up. For David, losing our dad was like the line to an anchor being cut, allowing my brother to begin a dangerous drift into rough seas.

David drank to deal with the pain — the pain of losing Dad, the pain of feeling like a failure, and the pain from his shattered ankle. The ankle he broke more than a decade earlier falling from a rope swing. The one he was too afraid to have fused. You could tell by the way he walked, dragging one leg behind him, that he lived in constant physical pain, and you could tell by the resentment in his voice and slur in his speech how much he'd had to drink.

My mom finally broke down and told me she had been helping pay David's mortgage almost every month since Dad died. Nearly five years. She was racking up debt and didn't know how to make ends meet. Things were going from bad to worse as David's drinking was becoming debilitating and depression was sinking its claws deeper.

He started lying to cover up his drinking and getting more

careless with his behavior, leaving empty Jack Daniels bottles in the basement of my mom's house.

When he was working, his drinking seemed to come under control a bit as he was up by five in the morning to be to a job site by six, and home after everyone had already eaten dinner. But work was tough to find. As a house painter, he was a hard worker when he could get work, but it was tough with unemployment rates in Michigan among the highest in the country.

He was laid off a few months out of the year. Mom's teacher salary wasn't enough to pay for two homes, so eventually David and his family moved in with Mom. There just didn't seem to be many options.

David seemed stuck. He just couldn't find a way to move forward through the pain.

An Acquired Taste

"The good Lord gave you a body that can stand most anything. It's your mind you have to convince."
VINCE LOMBARDI

So many people say they hate running. Heck, I've probably said it a million times. When I finished college football, I swore I would swear off two things — morning workouts and running. Most of us hate running. We are taught to hate it. It's used as punishment in P.E. class when we're kids, or by our coaches in sports. But there is another reason people hate running. They hate it because they aren't any good at it. They try it, and it's hard, so they quit.

That's how we respond to a lot of things in life, especially as adults. When we're kids, we're okay with being bad at something. If we like doing something, we'll keep doing it until we get good at it. But as we get older, we learn to fear failure. We become so afraid to fail that we start hating anything we can't be successful at right away.

Think about how many things you've heard people say they wish they could do, but don't.

"I wish I could play guitar. I wish I could get into better shape. I wish I could learn another language. I wish I could start a new business.

I wish, I wish, I wish.

But I don't."

Well, wishing doesn't cut it.

When people say they hate running, I say, "That's because you stink at it."

I pause and let them think that's it. I let it sink in.

"Did he just say I stink at running?"

Then I smile and say, "That's okay though. It's normal to stink at something when we first start trying it. And you can't get better at something if you're not willing to keep trying it for long enough for you to actually become better at it."

Like with anything, you need to start slowly. But with running, I mean that literally. If it's too hard, slow down. Take it one slow step at a time. Over time, you will get better. It may not get easy, but it will get easier. You may not love it right away, but you will begin to hate it less. And in time, you will begin to feel like a day is not complete unless you got to run. When I bought my first pair of running shoes I hated running, I dreaded every step. I rarely felt like going for a run, but I went anyway.

More than ten years later, there are still days I hate running, but I must admit, there are so many days I love it. It really is an acquired taste.

Runmotional

"If you want to win something, run 100 meters. If you want to experience something, run a marathon."

EMIL ZATOPEK

It's sort of hard to explain. The first few times you feel it, you can't figure out what's happening. I guess it's best to start at the beginning. At the root of it.

Where the feeling wells up from.

It starts on an ordinary day, usually when you're going about your life, business as usual. You can't put a finger on it. You certainly don't have the words for it. You may not even realize it's there. But, deep inside, you are hoping for something big.

Something new. Something that will change everything.

The first time you hear the idea, something triggers inside of you. Maybe it's a call from a friend. Maybe you see a poster on the subway train. Maybe you hear a commercial on the radio. Or maybe some guy is standing at the front of your church, on stage, talking about it. One thing is for sure, you did not wake up this morning expecting to sign up for a marathon.

But then it comes. The whisper. At first it's quiet but undeniable. You can't explain it. "You can't be talking to me," you tell this voice. "I've never run in my life. There is no way I could ever do this." But it's too late. You've heard it. You've felt it. And you know deep down, for some reason, that you are supposed to do this. You want to do this. You need to do this.

You are white-knuckling your chair, and fear comes on you fast. "I can't do this. There's just no way."

This is the point where so many will miss it, the opportunity of their life, to one day get the feeling — *runmotional.*

Sometimes once the decision is made, once the leap is taken, you get a taste of what it feels like. Butterflies fill your stomach as a rush of emotions floods your spirit, invades your mind. "I'm going to do this. I'm going to run this thing. I'm scared. What if I fail? I'm too old. Too young. Too out of shape. Too fat. Too sure that I'm supposed to do this to ignore this whisper."

Tears well in your eyes, and depending on your ability to maintain composure, you may or may not hold them back. That is, for now.

The months that follow present many more glimpses of it. But each one of them is only a foreshadowing of the real thing.

You walk into a running store to buy your first pair of real running shoes, frightened to death that they will laugh you right out of the store. You're afraid they'll say something like, "This one here thinks he's going to try to run a marathon!" But they don't say that. They smile and seem to know something you don't. They seem remarkably nonchalant about the whole thing. Rather pleasant in fact.

You stick to a plan that tells you how far to run each day.

It took you weeks to get up the courage to go to a group run. And as you pull into the parking lot to run with other people for the first time, the same fear comes back. "These people will laugh at me for sure. Maybe not to my face, but they'll be laughing all right. These folks are real runners." And again, you're surprised.

They welcome you as you pretend to understand the things they are talking about. The words they all seem to know.

"How was your tempo run this week?" "Whose got some Body Glide I can borrow?" "That's a sweet tech tee; where'd you get it?"

"Those Yasso's were brutal on Wednesday."

"Yeah, I skipped those and did fartleks instead."

They may as well be speaking a foreign language. And in the case of fartleks, they're literally speaking another language. But they all seem glad to have you there. You feel like a visitor here, but a welcomed one.

On nights before long runs, you lay in bed worrying whether you will be able to finish the run tomorrow. The longest run you've ever done. And this happens every week. Your longest run ever. Each week you get scared. And each week you feel like a champion as you overcome your fear.

There are obstacles along the way. Sometimes there are so many obstacles. People — discouraging you. Your body — uncooperative. Yourself — doubt.

The obstacles can feel insurmountable. But they usually aren't. When the day finally comes, you take inventory of everything but won't remember most of it. What you remember is the energy of that morning. People all around with bib numbers pinned to their shirts. Running hats, shorts, sunglasses, watches, compression socks, water belts with energy gels, and everyone heading in the same direction.

You are scared to death. A few months ago you would never have imagined this was possible. Not for you. But here you are walking to the starting line of your first marathon. And somehow, as terrified as you are, it all feels right.

You can't believe the crowd. "How can this many people be running this far today?

Have they all been through what I just went through? Six

months of early morning training runs before work? The blisters, aches, and pains? Did they face the same fear of failure and satisfaction of slow forward progress?"

Every single song that plays over the speakers gets you more amped than the one before. People are here for something special, and you are about to be a part of it. It feels so personal, but somehow it's okay that you're sharing this moment with thousands of strangers.

The first few miles go fast. You feel good. You can't believe how good you feel. How easy this feels. You couldn't be happier. Fans scream your name because it's written on your shirt. Some know exactly what it took for you to get here. Some have no idea.

By the midway point, you are starting to feel the miles take their toll. But you've been here before. You've gone this far in training. This part doesn't scare you much.

As you pass mile eighteen you realize mile twenty is coming. Past that is no-man's-land, the unknown. You begin wondering if the training plan was good enough. The farthest it took you was twenty miles. Everyone kept saying that was enough, twenty miles was all you needed to do. It didn't make sense. But what did you know? So you trusted them.

You pass the sign with two-zero on it. You're in deep now. The only way to the finish is to keep moving until you get there. No turning back.

Somewhere in this space is where it happens. For some it's sooner. For some, later.

But for most, this is the place where you feel it fully for the first time.

It starts in your gut and reaches deep into your soul. You might need to walk for a minute. You can't figure out what is going on. A rush of emotions comes over you, but you can't separate all of the feelings from one another. The first tear falls from your face to the street beneath you, and you ask yourself,

"Why am I crying?"

The answer is complicated. You're crying for so many reasons. You're crying because of all the fear you have walked through, just to take that first step, and all the fear that followed. You're crying because this was so much harder than you thought it would be, and so much better. You're crying because if you can do this, maybe there are a lot of other things you can do too. Things you're afraid of. You're crying, because everything is changed, even if you aren't exactly sure how or why. You're crying because you'll never be the same again.

Runmotional.

The Other Side

"Everything you ever wanted is on the other side of fear."

GEORGE ADDAIR

Almost every good thing in life, every plan God has in store for us, every dream, lies on the other side of fear. Fear drives us all from our dreams. Fear keeps most of us from doing what it is we were put on this earth to do.

After my dad died, I decided I wasn't going to wait until I was in my sixties to figure out what I was put here to do, my purpose. Those quiet times with God out on those runs had brought some relief to the pain I felt. Some clarity of thought.

I was still hurting, but I was beginning to trust God again. Maybe really for the first time. I knew this much: I wasn't going to waste this one life He gave me.

I spent a lot of time talking about my dreams with my mentor and friend Dr. Ron Brown. Ron had me make a list of everything I had ever wanted to be when I "grew up." Anything I ever dreamed of becoming. Everything was fair game.

After about a year I had, to some degree, narrowed it down. Here are some of the "dream-jobs" I had on my list:

1. Work for an advertising agency (I didn't even know what they did but I thought it sounded cool.)
2. Stand-up comedian (I do a pretty sweet Adam Sandler impression.)

3. Actor (I hadn't been in a play since the fifth grade.)
4. Personal Fitness Trainer (I had just lost 90 pounds and thought I could help others get fit too.)
5. Life Coach (Yep, I know what you're thinking. People pay for these?)

Once I had a list of some fairly clear ideas, Ron gave me an assignment: Choose the top three that might be my dream job, find someone who does that job and ask to spend a day with them.

I spent two days with different people who worked in advertising, visited two art schools and talked to all of my close friends trying to fully understand each of their jobs, to either rule them out or rule them in. I even researched how to get a joke on the "Tonight Show." Sadly, I couldn't come up with any funny jokes. I drew a line through stand-up comedian.

As I explored each of my dream jobs, I realized there were aspects of each one I liked, but I had idealized them all. I loved the creative aspects of advertising but couldn't see myself selling products I wouldn't use if you paid me. I liked aspects of several other "artistic" jobs but didn't like the solitude they required. With process of elimination as my only approach to chasing down my dreams, it seemed this might take a while.

Every time I met with Ron, he would ask me this one question before ending our time together: "Michael, what do you really want to do?" It was as if he could tell by the tone of my voice that something was missing. All of the dreams seemed nice, but there was no fire in my eyes or conviction in my voice when I talked about them.

My answer was always the same: "What I really want to do is to have an impact on global poverty, but I don't think I want to be a missionary. I guess I'll have to wait until later in life like my dad did to realize that part of my dream. I guess I'm not ready for whatever it is that I'm supposed to be doing. I guess chasing dreams is for kids. I guess there isn't more to this."

Guess again.

The Deep End

> *"If you want to learn to swim, jump into the water.*
> *On dry land no frame of mind is ever going to help you."*
>
> BRUCE LEE

A full Ironman consists of three endurance events. First, there's the swim. They call it the human washing machine. Over two thousand athletes all start in the water at the same time. A 2.4-mile open water swim with other athletes' limbs flailing about, smashing the water and you at the same time.

Second is the bike. When you get out of the water, you get on your bike and ride 112 miles. No drafting off of other cyclists.

And finally, there's the run. If you can still stand after you get off your bike, you tie up the laces on your running shoes and head out for a 26.2-mile run. Yep, after over an hour in the water, and upwards of six hours on a bike, you run a marathon.

My first thought when I heard about the Ironman triathlon? I'm in.

My second thought? I'd better learn how to swim.

I stood on the side of the pool more nervous than I had been since Little League baseball tryouts. I grew up with a pool in my backyard and spent a ton of time swimming in Lake Michigan, but I had never learned to swim. I could stay afloat, but I had no clue about proper swimming technique. I never learned to swim with my head down, breathing to either side, the way I had seen the Olympic swimmers do it. The way I knew it was supposed to be done. But, having signed up for an Ironman without already knowing how to swim, the day had come to jump into the deep end.

I knew I was about to make a fool of myself, but I had decided my fear of looking foolish would not keep me out of the water that day. I already felt silly wearing my new fitted swimsuit that looked like the bike shorts we wore under our junior high gym uniforms because the shorts were embarrassingly short. I may have already felt silly, but in just a minute, I was sure to look silly too.

The Olympic length pool at the University of Illinois athletic center where I was getting my Masters in Social Work was filled with swimmers who actually knew what they were doing, sliding through the water with ease and grace, rotating just enough to catch a breath of air, doing flip turns at each end of the fifty-meter pool, and doing all of it so effortlessly. I couldn't have looked more like a fish out of water than I did that day, ironically, in the water.

As I began to swim, I couldn't believe how out of breath I felt. My heart was racing, and having my face in the water made me feel like I was going to suffocate. It was a feeling that would take me months of practicing to get over. Beating the water with my flailing arms, splashing water like a trapped tuna caught in the nets, I was the picture of inefficiency in the water.

At one point I heard the lifeguard yelling, "Come here!" He seemed to be waving me over with his hand. Was I in trouble? Was I really such a bad swimmer that this guy was going to tell me so? I swam over to him fully expecting him to say something like, "Do you have any clue what you're doing? You look like an idiot flailing about like a dying fish. Just give it up, man."

Well, it wasn't as bad as I thought. I mean, I'm sure I did actually look like an idiot, but it turned out the guy wasn't even talking to me, he was just yelling to one of his friends. Embarrassed and relieved, I continued trying to swim with the sneaking suspicion he had actually called the other lifeguard over so they could laugh at the fool flailing about in the water like a wounded rainbow trout.

Looking back on that day I can hardly believe how nervous I was. It took a lot of work to learn to use proper technique. I borrowed a "Teaching Swimming" book from a friend of mine who was a gym teacher. I watched the other swimmers at the pool and tried to copy their form. And I had to work to overcome the extremely uncomfortable sensation of having my head underwater for any length of time, likely a by-product of my older brothers' trick with the kinked hose when I was three. But, the good news is, I can swim pretty well now.

I'm sure you've heard the saying, "You can't teach an old dog new tricks." If that's true then I think the key to not living out this cliché is to never become an old dog or at least don't act like one. Don't be afraid to try new things. Or rather, don't let the fear of trying new things keep you from doing it.

When I first started running, I didn't know a thing about what kind of shoes to buy, how fast I should be going, what a training schedule for a race looked like, or what a fartlek was. In fact, I was terrified to even go into the running store for fear of saying something stupid, not to mention being 265 pounds and worried they might laugh me out of the store. But I went anyway.

The same thing happened when I began swimming, and again when I started shopping for a bike for Ironman. Now, not *everyone* has this same fear of looking or sounding stupid. But in my experience most people do. What separates people is that some allow their fear to keep them from their dreams, while others walk through it.

I still feel scared when I am trying something new, but I am getting more and more used to the feeling, and more confident in overcoming it. The butterflies in my stomach are still there, and I still feel a bit *stupid* when I don't know what I'm doing. I may get embarrassed asking questions that might sound silly to the *experts*. I'm becoming accustomed to the process, the journey through fear. I may even be getting used to it. It's always worth going through the fear to get to the good stuff.

The Ride of My Life

*"Let my heart be broken by the things that break
the heart of God."*

BOB PIERCE, FOUNDER OF WORLD VISION

Just a couple of months from attempting my first Ironman and less than two years after running my first marathon, Mark Smith called with heartbreaking news. His one-year old daughter, Olivia, had been diagnosed with leukodystrophy, a degenerative brain disease. According to doctors, the tissues in her brain would slowly break down until she lost all motor skills, her body would stop working, and she would die, likely before reaching age three or four.

Mark had just started attending church and understanding God's love for us. I worried what this might do to his faith. To his wife, Tamera. I could hear the fear in his voice over the phone. I knew the pain of losing my dad. How it destroyed me. But this, losing a child. I couldn't find the words.

The next day after Mark's call, I dedicated my eighty-five mile training bike ride, my longest ever, to praying for Olivia. It would take me five lonely hours to cover eighty-five miles and alone on the road was the best place I had found to spend time with God. Maybe the only time I truly spent with God.

As I started my ride with the rising sun early that Saturday, I settled into a cadence that would need to be sustained through head winds, the July summer heat, and that Midwest humidity. With stalks of corn as my only spectators, and occasional passing cars my only competition, I took full advantage of being the only cyclist on the roads, of being alone. It isn't often I spend time by myself. Training for that race brought the longest periods of solitude I can remember ever having, before or since.

Early into my ride, I began praying for Olivia. I had told myself I would devote my entire ride to her. It wasn't long before the bartering started. I should have recognized it. This making deals with God thing. This trying to bend His will to mine. I would catch myself praying, "God, you can't do this. You have to change this. God, give it to me, Mark can't take this." And then, I clearly remember praying, and taking it back as soon as the words formed in my mind, "God, take this from Olivia and give it to my child one day. The child that I'll have some day. Give this to my child, and take it from Mark's. From Olivia."

As soon as I uttered these prayers, I was struck with fear, as though God might agree to my bartering, as if I have that type of influence on the plans of the Creator. I acted like God was waiting for me to pray this so He could heap a little more pain on my head, break my heart again. Here I was, praying again, but still believing God was out to get me. That He had something other than love for me. Something that required I make some sort of deal with Him, as though I had something of worth to offer.

Despite my best intentions to pray for Olivia for the entire duration of my lonely ride, it wasn't long before my A.D.D. kicked in and my mind began to wander, away from this precious little girl for whom my heart was breaking. Somehow, I kept praying the scattered prayers of a brokenhearted dreamer whose faith was on the mend.

It was on that five-hour bike ride that I had what I can only describe as a vision from God. "What if I dedicated my next race to raising money to help kids in other countries, poor countries? Kids like the ones I met in Haiti. Kids like the ones I saw in the commercials when I was young. The kids I had long dreamed about helping."

What? Was God really speaking this clearly to me? It was the most personal experience with God I had ever had. It was like He was painting a picture in my mind and connecting it to a passion in my heart, clearly laying out for me a plan that simply needed to be executed. At first it was vague, the way the background of a painting lacks details in many places, and then the details began to fill themselves in.

At every race, people litter the course with pink, yellow, and purple jerseys, representing myriad charities for which people race and raise money. Surely, I thought, there was already someone doing this, using races to help the poorest people in the world. But as I racked my brain, I could not remember seeing any at the races I'd been to. Certainly I would have noticed them. My heart was beating faster than my riding speed should have required. My mind was racing faster than usual. This idea, this was it. I knew beyond any doubt this was the dream God had planted in my heart, that this was what I was supposed to do with my life.

By the end of the bike ride, I knew I would I dedicate my next race to helping children in poor countries, and that God was telling me to get others to join me. Hundreds, maybe even thousands, of others to join me.

I don't remember putting my bike away that day and I barely remember the ride, as hours seemed to pass in minutes with the ideas coming so fast and clear. The second I got home, I went into my office at Campus Life and wrote down every idea that had come to me on my ride. The ideas came fully and freely, effortless.

They weren't mine. They had been entrusted to me.

When I told my best friend, Timmy, about the vision I had on that ride, he said, "Michael, you've got to find the best organization that is helping people in these countries, and share your idea with them."

So that's what I did.

I researched humanitarian organizations to find out who was doing great work. And by research I mean I "Googled" it. World Vision came up at or near the top of every list of great organizations, and I discovered they were one of the largest humanitarian organizations in the world, and they had an office in Chicago, just a couple of hours north of where we were living.

A guy named Mike Mantel headed up the Chicago office, so I gave him a call. It went straight to voice mail. The message I left went something like this. "Mr. Mantel. My name is Michael Chitwood. I have an idea for you. An idea on how to raise a bunch of money to help kids around the world. If you'd like to hear my idea, give me a call back. Thanks."

Sixty seconds later my phone rang. It was Mike Mantel. He wanted to hear my idea. After giving him a two-minute version of what I considered to be the best idea ever, I asked, "So what do you think? Are you interested?"

And this part I remember almost word for word.

"Michael, I'm interested in anything that can bring more help to kids. If you're ever in Chicago, let me know and we can grab a cup of coffee."

Our call ended shortly after that.

I couldn't sleep that night. It couldn't wait. I called him back the next day. "Mr. Mantel. I'll be in Chicago tomorrow. Can we meet?"

The next day I sat across from Mike Mantel in the World Vision office in Chicago. I slid him a proposal, and he pushed it to the side without even looking at it, and said, "So tell me more about this idea."

After a thirty-minute meeting, I was pretty sure he was hooked. But it was still a long way from Mike Mantel liking my idea to me joining the World Vision crew. After my meeting with him, I told Dani, and my mentor, Ron, "I'll do this for free if they'll let me." I knew World Vision was where God wanted me to land with this dream He had handed me.

Mike Mantel connected me with Dana Buck, who worked for World Vision in the national office just outside of Seattle. Dana and a couple of other World Vision folks had actually been laying the groundwork for the exact same dream, a program that would empower individuals to run in races and raise money for World Vision's work in Africa. Dana, Laurie Humphreys, and Karen Kartes had been working on this idea and had been trying to find a way to give it legs, so to speak.

The day after I met with Mike Mantel, I was at O'Hare airport waiting to fly to a wedding in Florida when I got a return call from Dana. We laughed as I shared my ideas with him and he literally finished my sentences, it was almost scary. We had even chosen the exact same name for this program: Team World Vision.

Soon after, Mike Mantel had me meet with Amber Johnson, the last person who would have to be convinced this thing might actually work. If they were going to give me a shot, she would be my new boss. I drove up for the meeting despite Amber insisting we could just talk on the phone, and it's a good thing I did. She later told me the reason she had insisted I not make the drive was she had already decided she didn't think the idea would work and didn't want to waste my time. By the time I left her office, I was pretty sure she was in.

A few weeks after that five-hour bike ride, when I had failed to continually pray for Olivia, where God had given me a dream that would change my life, I got another call from Mark. They had taken Olivia to several of the best hospitals around the country, one in Michigan, and the world famous Mayo Clinic in Minnesota. After weeks of worrying, and heartache, and praying, and crying, they were told that the original diagnosis of leukodystrophy was wrong. Olivia actually had muscular dystrophy.

Can you imagine being relieved to hear your two-year-old daughter has muscular dystrophy? You would be if you knew there were more terrible things, more painful things, more hopeless things for a child to have. Olivia would face a lot of challenges in her life, the doctors had told them, but she would be okay.

Mark told me the doctors said they must have made a mistake. "But," he told me, "how do they know Olivia didn't actually have leukodystrophy, but God changed it? How could they be sure this wasn't actually a miracle?"

A Marathon's Mean Big Brother

"People of mediocre ability sometimes achieve outstanding success because they don't know when to quit. Most men succeed because they are determined to."

GEORGE ALLEN

If you are running a marathon, on a perfect day, you can make it through the entire race feeling pretty good. It is actually possible to get to the finish line without hitting "the wall," although it's unlikely on most days. But if something goes wrong, you might just have to gut it out feeling less than good.

The Ironman is like a marathon in so many ways, but still so different. In fact, it's more than *like* a marathon; it's like a marathon's mean big brother. When I signed up for my first Ironman, I got some incredibly useful, if a bit alarming, advice from a random guy I met who had done several Ironman races.

"You're going to feel like crap," he told me very matter-of-factly.

What? That doesn't sound like the encouragement I needed from an experienced Ironman athlete. That's not how runners talk to each other. We encourage each other. "You can do it!" And all that feel-good stuff. Then here's this guy, this Ironman, telling me I'm going to feel worse than I've ever felt.

"At some point in the race, probably more than once, you *will* feel terrible," he said emphatically. "Stomach problems, a bad headache, dizziness, cramping. It's Ironman. It's a looooonnnnnggg race, which means it's a long day, which means you *will* feel like crap at some point. The reason I'm telling you this is so you can be ready. Don't expect that you'll feel great all day. It's not likely to happen.

That's the bad news: at some point, you will feel horrible. You'll probably even feel like quitting. You might give it more consideration than you ever have before. Don't quit. There is good news too. It will pass. Yes, you will feel terrible at some point. Probably worse than you ever thought you could feel. But, at some point, you will begin to feel a little better, and then a little more. At some point, it will pass."

"Now, just to be clear," he continued, "it will likely come back. Maybe not the exact same problem. If you had a headache early in the race, you might have bad bathroom issues later. It might not look the same, but you will feel the same. Like crap. Remember. It will pass. Things will get better again. You won't feel this terrible forever. Just for a while. If you can keep that in mind, you can get through those tough spots. Just keep telling yourself 'this will pass.'"

I started to wonder if this stranger was still telling me what to expect in an Ironman or in grief. I had learned that life has more pain in store for me than I would have ever dreamed possible. I knew what it meant to come on bad times. I had learned that though my grief would never fully leave, I wouldn't always feel the intensity of it as frequently as I was then. Things would get better again. I wouldn't always feel this terrible. This too shall pass.

At the same time, I wondered, who signs up for this stuff? Why would anyone willingly subject himself to the type of pain and discomfort this stranger told me I'd feel? Maybe, just maybe, if every good thing lies on the other side of fear and pain, what he was telling me could be true. There could be rewards on the other side of my pain that I could never have imagined while I was enduring the full intensity of it.

Tough to Watch

"Don't stop — people are watching."

IRONMAN SPECTATOR SIGN

DNF means "Did Not Finish." That's what appears next to your name in the results listing if you start a race and, for any reason, fail to cross the finish line in the allotted time, which for an Ironman is 17 hours.

At my first Ironman, 21 percent of the field did not finish. Of the 2,076 people who went into Lake Monona that morning, only 1,678 made it across the finish line, three more finished just after the 17-hour cutoff, and 398 did not finish. And 202 didn't even complete the 112-mile bike course. It was a tough day, 91 degrees with a heat index over 100.

The start line of Ironman is one of the most electrifying places on planet earth. If a marathon start line is like an electric power line, imagine a downed power line that touches a lake with 2,000 people wading in, readying themselves for flailing arms and legs, thrashing through the water, and making lots of unintentional contact with other people's faces. The swim was complete chaos as 2,000 people swam the double-loop 2.4-mile course in Lake Monona next to, in front of, behind, and on top of one another. At the beginning I was surprised how much it didn't feel like swimming but more like trying not to drown. But about a half-mile in, I began to find my groove.

As we came out of the water we realized that it was going to be a hot day. Volunteers lathered the athletes with sunscreen and sent us off on our bikes — 112 miles of hills lay ahead.

On the bike course, people were dropping like flies. The bodies strewn across the landscape looked like a war zone as people lay motionless on the ground beside the road waiting for the sag wagons to pick them up. The temperature was in the mid-nineties and it was taking its toll. For some reason, I felt surprisingly strong. I think I was just so happy to be there.

I found myself trying to encourage the other athletes as we traded places passing one another. I would yell to the folks laying in the grass next to their bikes that I was praying for them. One guy passed me and yelled, "Hey Chitwood," reading my name from my bib, "I got back on my bike because of you. Thanks for praying for me!"

The bike course is a double loop, which means that every big hill you climb, you have to climb again. I didn't do so great the second time around. Loop two took almost an hour longer than loop one. I was slowing down a ton. At mile seventy, I suffered a tough blow. I had been looking forward to seeing my family again where I had seen them on loop one. In fact, it was the thing that was keeping me going, climbing those giant hills. I just kept telling myself, "Hold on, you will see them soon." And then, they weren't there.

It's amazing how much seeing your loved ones can encourage you in tough times. And it can be devastating when you are expecting support and it isn't there. Often people don't realize how much of a difference they can make in your life just being there for you when you're hitting a rough patch.

Luckily my family hadn't abandoned me. They had repositioned themselves so they wouldn't miss me at the bike-to-run transition. After you swim 2.4 miles and bike 112, it is with mixed emotions that you lace up your running shoes. On one hand you are so glad to not be on the bike. On the other, there's that pesky 26.2-mile run you still have to do.

My legs felt like lead for the first few miles, but they loosened up and I felt pretty good through the first half. But, the start of that second loop was one of the toughest parts of any race I've ever done. As I was nearing the turn for loop two, I could see the Capitol building in the distance, the finish line. As I made the turn, I could see several athletes skip the turn and keep running straight towards the finish line. They were, apparently, finishing loop two, I was just beginning it, 13.1 miles to go.

The run brought some relief from the heat as the sun was going down by the time I hit the second loop of the marathon course. I walked a lot during that second half, especially during the later miles. It was dark out. It was lonely. But I felt good. I knew I would finish.

I crossed the finish line completely satisfied and thoroughly exhausted, in 14 hours, 9 minutes, and 1 second, in 939th place. Twenty-one percent of the people who started the race that day did not cross the finish line. The biggest DNF in Ironman history.

After the congratulatory hugs from Dani, my mom, and my brother Dan, I asked, "Where's Timmy with the car?"

"Oh, we sent him to get pizza. We're all starving."

"How are we getting back to his house?"

"Well, we figured we could walk, it's just over a mile from here."

Were they serious? They wanted me to walk, with my bike, after finishing a fourteen-hour race? Oh, yes. They were serious. So, despite being completely spent, I pushed my own bike down the hill from the Monona Terrace, past the Capitol and along the unlit side streets back to Timmy's place.

When he finally arrived with the pizza (which truly was a good idea even though they should have had it delivered), my mom said, out loud, "That was a tough day."

"What do you mean?" I asked. "Tough for you?" thinking she might be kidding.

"Yeah. It was hot. And it was so long. That was tough to watch."

It's true that being a spectator at long-distance sporting events requires its own brand of endurance. People have to be deeply committed to you to want to follow your progress and support you through all of the ups and downs for up to seventeen hours. I knew what my mom had said was true.

And supporting someone in their pain, grief, and loss, through all of the ups and downs this entails, can leave you feeling the way my mom felt after my first Ironman — worn out and tired.

As I have endured deep grief over the losses in my life, there have been few people who have known how to stay with me on the course. It's exhausting watching someone be high one day and rock bottom in his grief the next.

I love when my family comes to cheer me on at marathons or Ironman events, and their support empowers me to endure one more step, one more mile. But I also know now that no one will ever fully meet my expectations for being with me in my pain, whether I'm enduring an Ironman challenge or a wall of pain in my heart.

Team World Vision

"I am not called to be successful. I am called to be faithful."

MOTHER TERESA

I had no clue what I was doing. I sat down at my desk on my first day, January 4, 2006, with no real idea how to do this thing I had just convinced World Vision to hire me to do. But I knew I was supposed to do it, the way a bird knows it's supposed to fly south for the winter, the only difference being birds actually know what they're doing. I may have felt called to do this, but I never stopped to think if I would know *how* it would be done.

Just four months after doing my first Ironman, I had moved to Chicago and was living with my friend Joe. Dani still had a semester of grad school left, so we would see each other on the weekends. It hadn't been an easy decision. Sure, we had talked about moving to Chicago someday down the road, but this came fast, from an idea on a bike ride to moving to Chicago in just a few months.

We shed a lot of tears during the weeks and months leading up to my move. Dani supported me every step of the way, but we both knew it was going to be pretty tough to live in separate cities for three and a half months. We figured we knew what we were getting into and were ready to take it on. But living apart proved to be much tougher than I could have imagined. The learning curve at World Vision was steep, especially since I was the first person to ever do my job. I pray we never have to do that again.

On day one in the new job, I sat down at my desk at the World Vision office in Chicago and couldn't help but think, "What the heck did I get myself into? I don't have a clue what I am doing."

Just four months earlier, I had convinced my new boss, Amber, to hire me, to let me help start Team World Vision and recruit people to run in the Chicago Marathon. Other than my friend Joe, whom I was living with, I didn't know a soul in Chicago and had no idea where to start.

I was pretty stoked when one of the older guys at the office, Louie, asked me to lunch on my second day. Louie was in his late fifties and had been working as a fundraiser with World Vision's big donors for a long time. He suggested we go to MacArthur's, a soul food diner on the west side of Chicago not far from the World Vision office. We made small talk on the short ride there, and Louie seemed interested in what I had to say, although a bit pragmatic and maybe a little crotchety. He walked me through the ordering process at MacArthur's counter as he told me what foods they were best known for and what to avoid.

We grabbed a table in the crowded restaurant and sitting across from me he said, "Okay, so tell me about this thing you're trying to do."

I spent the next fifteen minutes casting the vision for what Team World Vision would become. How I was going to try to get hundreds, maybe even thousands of people to run marathons and raise money for World Vision's work. How running had changed my life. Restored my faith. Healed my soul. How I really believed running could change anyone's life, and we could do it all to raise money to support World Vision's work in Africa.

When I was done with what I considered to be a compelling speech, Louie paused to make sure I was done talking, set his Diet

Coke down, looked me dead in the eyes and said, "It will never work."

Gulp. Pit in stomach. What did I get myself into?

He listed all the flaws in my plan, spelling out every obstacle he thought I would face, how these obstacles would prove to be too difficult, and that in the end, this Team World Vision thing would simply fail. "It will never work," he said one more time, maybe for effect.

Maybe he was just a grumpy old man. Maybe he was testing me, trying to see if I had what it would take. Maybe it was his version of hazing; he was a retired Navy veteran after all. Maybe he was serious. Maybe he was right. Maybe it wouldn't work. Maybe it couldn't.

But maybe it could.

Despite the risk of failure, I had to be faithful to the dream God put in my heart.

Part Two: Between One Loss and Another

My dad and his mom.

My dad as a school teacher back in the day.

My dad and I, back to back, my 2nd birthday.

My dad and I, back to back, my 21st birthday.

My brothers as little kids.

My brothers and I. David, left, Dan, right, and me in the headlock.

My mom, brothers, and I. (Dan on the end and David next to me).

My brothers Dan, left, and Dave having a mud fight as kids.

My wife, Dani, and I just having fun.

Dani and I with Josphine, Maurine, and their family
- Shadrack, Millicent, Astone, Elias, Jacqueline.
Not pictured: Justine and Japheth.

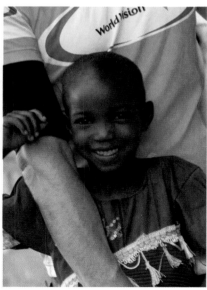

My wife, Dani, and I.   *Maurine.*

Maurine and I.

Josh Cox, Andy Baldwin, and I with our World Vision sponsored children Rodgers, Cosmos, and Maurine.

My friends and I getting runmotional: Top left: Steve Spear and I halfway through his run from LA to NY. Top right: Rusty and I at the finish line of our 100-mile run. Bottom left: Thad Sweet and I at the finish of Comrades 2010. Bottom right: Tim Hoekstra and I halfway through his 50-mile run.

Rusty, Paul JVR, Hannah and I at the start line of our 100-mile run.

The empty start of the Chicago Marathon on our 100-mile run.

Dani with me at the finish line of our 100-mile run.

Top photo: 1000 Rockstars – Team World Vision runners at the start of the 2010 Chicago Marathon. Bottom left: Team World Vision Kenya. Bottom right: 100 Rock Stars – Team World Vision at the 2006 Chicago Marathon.

Mud Man

"There is still one thing you haven't done," he told him. "Go and sell all your possessions and give the money to the poor, and you will have treasure in heaven. Then come, follow me."

JESUS CHRIST

I was scared about my first trip to Africa. Not scared about my safety, scared about what might happen inside me. Scared that God was going to ask me to give up everything I had for the poor. And there would only be two possible outcomes. Obey Him and be miserable. Or disobey Him and be miserable. Just those two options. And the thought of having to choose either one scared me. I was bound to fail.

I had been at World Vision for just six months and was learning so much about the way they help communities holistically, tackling the root causes of poverty and finding sustainable solutions. It all looked so good on paper, but sometimes I wondered if it was too good to be true. Did it really work this well? Here was my opportunity to find out.

The World Vision Ethiopia staff included some of the most talented people I had ever met. Men and women with college degrees who could be working in developed cities but instead had chosen to live and work as water engineers, agricultural engineers, and health care specialists in the poorest communities in the world, serving the poor.

After visiting the rural communities in Ethiopia where World Vision works, we spent a couple of days in the capital city of Addis Ababa. We visited the open market, one of the largest in the world. Just before heading back to our hotel, I saw a man out of the corner of my eye.

He was lying on the ground on his stomach, begging. He was obviously crippled, his entire body affected. I could barely see his eyes, as he could not lift his head up that far. He was covered in dirt and mud. His legs were a mangled mess of deformity. His body bent and twisted in the middle so he could not stand up even if his legs had worked. His spirit seemed broken. No one appeared to even notice he was there.

Foreigners are generally encouraged not to give money to beggars, to not promote dependence. After we passed, I checked with my new friend Tamiru from World Vision Ethiopia whether it was considered acceptable to give money to people with disabilities. He told me it was okay because in Ethiopia there are no other options for a person with this severe of a disability except to beg. They have usually been disregarded by family, neighbors, and society as cursed. They truly are the poorest of the poor, the most vulnerable of the most vulnerable.

I felt ashamed to approach him, like I wasn't worthy to even talk to him. I was embarrassed by my privilege. What had I done to deserve a working body? What had I done to earn my status as a citizen of the richest country in the history of the world? I knelt down next to him and he took my hand and began to kiss it repeatedly as I gave him 100 Birr (not even $10 U.S.). I prayed with him, kissed his dirty hand, and my eyes welled with tears as I left him. For the rest of the day, I couldn't stop thinking about how Jesus responded to people like this man. I believe he would do much more, and he expects much more from us.

Later that night, I lay in my comfortable bed in my hotel room and thought about that man and how he was most likely still out on the street, or trying to pull his lame body underneath whatever type of shelter he may be able to find, a cardboard box or a piece of corrugated metal held up by some sticks. This was his reality. This was his life every day and likely had been for many years.

This man was only one of many like him I saw on the trip. There were many others as we drove along the rocky dirt roads, and I felt the quick jolt of sympathy when seeing them. But then I turned my eyes and mind from the sight, I think as a defense mechanism, realizing how hard the truth of their existence is. How hard the truth of my own inaction and the inaction of others is.

These were the people Jesus taught us to help. When everyone else pushed away the lepers, he touched them, and loved them. By not acknowledging these people — by not acting to help them, by turning my mind and eyes because I felt afraid of the implications on my own life, what obligations acknowledging them may bring — I knew I was disobeying God.

There is hope for the man in the mud. That hope is people like you and me just being willing to not walk past, not look away and ignore his hurt, but to care enough to do something to help.

100 Rock Stars

"As a rock star, I have two instincts, I want to have fun, and I want to change the world. I have the chance to do both."

BONO

The night before the 2006 Chicago Marathon, we gathered 100 people in the basement of a church for our first pre-race team dinner. These people had been the first to join the team, the first to take on the challenge of a marathon to help fund clean water projects in Kenya.

To support World Vision's work in communities like the ones I had been to in Ethiopia, the first to share the dream with me. There had been a handful of individuals — Mark Wagner, Tim Hoekstra, and Bethany Jones — who, during the years before Team World Vision started, ran and raised money for World Vision. But now we were a team, a family. God had not only given this dream to me, He had planted the seed in hundreds of peoples' hearts, maybe even thousands. People, who, like me, longed to change the world and have fun in the process.

Mike Mantel, the guy that hired me, took it personally and signed up to run with the team. My new boss, Amber Johnson, and Lauren Wilgus, who was on the World Vision marketing team, gave countless hours of support to Team World Vision. My friend Marc Valadez took on huge responsibilities with Team World Vision, overseeing the race day experience. And at our first events, guess who was the first person there to help and the last one to leave? Louie. Yep, Mr. "This Will Never Work" became one of Team World Vision's biggest supporters.

The best advice someone ever gave me about growing Team World Vision was this:

"Make sure everyone on the team feels like a rock star."

It isn't hard to make them feel like rock stars, because, in our eyes that's exactly what they are.

Iron-Dan

"When things go wrong, don't go with them."

ELVIS PRESLEY

My brother, Dan, had locked himself in a porta-potty and was seriously contemplating never coming out. He had reached a breaking point and found refuge in a filthy, stinky, plastic box that reeked of the nastiest stench imaginable.

Three years earlier, when Dan came to watch my first Ironman, he said, "One day, maybe in ten or fifteen years when my kids are grown, I'll consider doing an Ironman with you."

With four kids, there just didn't seem to be a way to train for Ironman. Three years later though, he was wading into the cold waters of Lake Monona in Madison, Wisconsin, with me, waiting for the starting gun to go off for his first Ironman.

Dan didn't want to sacrifice family time, so he did a lot of his bike rides on a trainer in their living room, watching movies with his kids. He did some of his long runs on a one-mile loop around his neighborhood. The kids would take turns running laps with him. His oldest daughter, Taylor, was twelve. His sons, Payton and Jordan, were nine and eleven. And his daughter Danni was just seven at the time. (Yes, it gets confusing with Dani my wife, Dan my brother, and Danni my niece.)

Dan always outperformed his natural ability in sports. In football he got a college scholarship as a five-ten, two-hundred-pound middle linebacker. He was too small for his position but made up for it in heart and hard work. Like me, running and triathlon filled a void in his life he hadn't even realized was there.

His build was still that of a middle linebacker, and despite his strict training plan, he knew he had to work his plan just right if he hoped to make the seventeen hour cutoff time.

He came out of the water in good time and felt great all day on the bike. He was sticking to his plan, which would get him done with plenty of time to finish the marathon portion of the Ironman. But trouble set in late on the bike course when he was encouraging another rider he had been passing back and forth all day.

"Come on Julie, we've got this," he yelled to her, reading the name on her race bib.

"Dan, we're never going to make it." Julie shouted back, her voice breaking.

"Sure we are, I feel good. You look great. I'm telling you, we've got this!"

"Dan, we're not going to make the bike cutoff," she said.

That's when he realized the hole in his plan. Dan had planned his day perfectly, accounting for the level of effort he could afford to put into each event based on his training so he could make the final cutoff. What he had completely forgotten to plan for was the cutoff time for each individual event.

Having averaged just thirteen miles per hour to this point, he would need to average nineteen mph for the rest of the biking portion just to finish before the bike cutoff. If he didn't, they wouldn't even allow him to start the run. This realization came to him while riding through the town of Verona. He still had Hell Hill and Mt. Horrible.

You work the plan until the plan stops working. When the plan stops working, you get a new plan. "Hammer down!" he told himself, hoping Julie would hear him and follow suit.

Those remaining miles on the bike demanded everything he had, but he made it to the transition just minutes before the bike cutoff. As quickly as he could, Dan laced up his running shoes and headed out for the run.

Because the marathon course at Ironman Wisconsin loops back on itself multiple times, I got to see Dan out on the run. I thought he looked pretty good. He forced a smile and at least a couple of encouraging words back to me as we ran past one another on opposite sides of the street. I knew he would feel a bit deflated when he realized I was on my final loop and he was on his first. But when I saw him he looked strong and gave me some encouragement. Little did I know just how defeated he felt, which brings us back to that stinky porta-potty he had locked himself in.

"Maybe I should just stay inside this porta-potty until the race is over. No one will even care," Dan told himself.

He later told me how surprised he was by the voice that almost convinced him to quit. "It's not a screaming voice in your face yelling at you, I could deal with that. That's just my college football coach. No, it's much worse than that. It's a quiet whisper. 'Just quit. You can't do it.' "

That whisper comes to us all sometimes, the one telling us to give up, the one telling us that we can't do it, it's not worth it, we're not worth it.

And there in that stinky porta-potty, ready to give up, Dan understood a little bit of what it felt like to be desperate, to feel hopeless. The guy who always persevered was on the edge of quitting.

"I realized why people give up," he told me. "Why people quit. Life just breaks them."

But he didn't stay in that porta-potty. He didn't quit. He came out and kept moving forward, one step at a time. He got himself unstuck, and when the race clock read 16 hours, 29 minutes, 10 seconds, Dan heard the words over the loud speaker: "Dan Chitwood, you are an IRONMAN!"

Later, Dan told me, "I wanted God to make it easy. Instead, He gave me the ability to endure."

We all have our porta-potty moments, times when life stinks and we aren't sure we can keep going. We feel like giving up. Desperate, hopeless, that quiet voice whispers in our ear, *"Just quit, you can't do it, you're not worth it, nobody cares."* All we want is for God to make the pain go away, to make life easier.

Knowing these moments will come can help prepare us to deal with them. But perhaps of greater importance is our ability to recognize these moments in others, to seize the opportunity to knock on the door of whatever porta-potty they're stuck in and simply ask, "Hey, everything okay in there?"

Running for Life

"I was thirsty, and you gave me something to drink."
JESUS CHRIST

The sun was high as noon neared on this middle-of-October day, the end of the dry season in Zambia. Race organizers scurried about, making final preparations before the start of the event. They assembled us in ten single file lines by age, and a few men came around stapling pieces of paper the size of note cards to our shirts on the front and back. Each piece of paper had a number written on it with a Sharpie marker. They stapled them. To our shirts. With a stapler.

What were they doing stapling these numbers to our shirts? Didn't they know you don't just go around stapling numbers to people? The men looked at me as though I should be expecting this, this stapling of the numbers to our shirts. These were, of course, our race numbers. And the ten single-file lines we were standing in were the starting line of the race.

Distance running is not a huge sport in Zambia. Not the way it is in Kenya or Ethiopia. My first clue was the drive to the start line. We kept going downhill. It slowly dawned on me what this meant: the course they had plotted out for the race would be uphill — fifteen kilometers of running (just over nine miles), uphill the entire way.

There were about 100 of us at the start line, from children no older than seven or eight, to some of the village elders well into their sixties. With me stood Ryan and Sara Hall, two of the most famous American runners. I watched in amazement as their hand-written race numbers were stapled to their shirts. Just eight weeks earlier, Ryan had run the marathon for the U.S. team at the Olympics in Beijing. Sara leaned over to him and said something to the effect of, "You don't need to win you know. Just have fun and let one of the kids win." The sign held up by Ryan and Sara Hall at the starting line read:

Muselle ADP Community
In conjunction with World Vision Team (Chicago)
Proudly presents
A Marathon from Jiwunu to Kisasa
Theme: Water for Life
Run for Safe Water (life run)

We were there to visit the work World Vision was doing alongside communities in Zambia. It was clear the community of Muselle had never put on a race before, but they had definitely seen certain aspects of them. They had all the right components: a starting line, bib numbers, aid station. Everything was off just a bit, but different in a way that was endearing — the ten rows of single-file lines at the start, the handwritten bib numbers stapled to us, a makeshift aid station, and a finish line at a well.

The starting line was at a school World Vision had worked with the community to build and equip. The students were so proud they had a school to go to.

As the race started, we headed down a dirt path some vehicles drove on, but I would hardly call it a road.

Within a quarter-mile, I noticed two little girls who looked about seven or eight but were likely ten or eleven had settled into a pace right next to me. One was wearing socks pulled up nearly to her knees but no shoes. The other had bare feet covered in dirt and appeared to have never felt the comfort of a shoe. It was difficult to tell their actual age because often children in these rural African communities have stunted growth due to malnutrition.

They ran next to me with great intentionality. If I slowed, they slowed, and they would look up at me as if to say, "Hey dude, why are we slowing down, isn't this a race?"

The road was more like a dirt trail through the bush. It twisted and turned as we headed out toward the main road where we would begin a long uphill run. The two girls stayed with me stride for stride.

We watched as other people from the village slowed their runs to walks while others passed us. An old man wearing big black boots was hunched over as he ran. Women who were likely great grandmothers moved along the course slowly. It was obvious this was the first time they had been in a race, and I wondered what motivated them to participate that day.

When I saw the men with machine guns standing in the road, it didn't cause me too much alarm. There are men with guns everywhere in Africa — security guards, policemen, gas station attendants. I later learned Ryan Hall was completely freaked out when the men with guns approached him and snatched the bib number from his shirt, leaving the one on his back. This was the checkpoint, their version of the timing mat, the assurance that no one could cut the course short and cheat. Being the U.S. Olympian and the fastest American marathoner ever, Ryan certainly didn't need to cut the course short.

The machine guns didn't seem odd, but seeing the security

force holding out water bottles did. This was obviously the water station we had been promised. The people of Muselle had worked hard to make this a real race.

As we headed up the long road, my two little friends looked fatigued. They were working hard. Every few minutes I would look down, and they would look back into my eyes. I saw such seriousness in their gaze. While they only looked to be eight or nine, their eyes held a lifetime's worth of pain. These were the girls who had spent their days walking in search of water, filling jerry cans that weigh forty pounds when full with dirty water that would make them sick, missing school, forgoing their childhoods, risking their lives each day. My heart broke for them. These were the children we had been running for, and not just today and not just us, but every time we put on our Team World Vision jerseys at a race back home with all the teammates who run with us.

Just as I started wondering if we had made a wrong turn, if we would ever reach the end of this race, I began to hear the sounds of a finish line. Song. The air was filled with song. Hundreds of people from the village lined the road cheering for us in Bemba and accented English as we approached the finish line. Just then, both of my little friends found renewed energy and took off, sprinting to the finish. I didn't have it in me to run any faster.

"No, wait for me," I yelled to them as I reached out for their little hands. They obliged and each put their hand in mine. Tears filled my eyes, and I laughed out loud with joy at how rare this experience was. My two little friends ran with me hand in hand to the finish line. They hugged me and we all sat down in the dirt, exhausted.

The finish line was right at one of the new water points where World Vision and the community had just completed a deep borehole well. It was the greatest finish line of any race I've ever run. I doubt I'll ever see my two little running partners again this side of heaven, but they will stay in my heart forever.

The day finished with one of the most memorable moments of any trip I've taken to Africa. While the village elders and the World Vision staff showed us how the pump worked, something caught my eye about fifty yards away. Two little girls were getting water from one of the wells we were there to celebrate. No one was watching them but me. Far from the finish line and celebration, away from the fanfare and the foreigners, these two girls were filling their jerry cans with clean water. Water that would not make them sick. Water that was close to home. Water that would make it possible for them to go to school. Water that had changed their lives.

Team World Vision was running to raise money for clean water, and what we were doing was changing lives.

Part Two: Between One Loss and Another

Pain Management

> *"Pain insists upon being attended to. God whispers to us in our pleasures, speaks in our consciences, but shouts in our pains. It is His megaphone to rouse a deaf world."*
>
> C.S. LEWIS

It's going to hurt. You just have to face the fact that it's going to hurt, bad. A new kind of pain. One you've never felt before. Discouraging pain. Debilitating pain. Pain that casts doubt on your best efforts and reinforces your worst fears. This is going to hurt.

Whether you're training for a marathon or trying to endure a loss, it's about pain management. You can't put it completely out of your mind. The pain is there, and it won't let you simply cast it aside and forget about it completely. So you are forced to deal with it, and there are a lot of ways you try.

Sometimes you pretend. Pretend it doesn't hurt at all. You just keep telling yourself, "I feel okay. Wow, this isn't so bad. It doesn't really hurt that much. It's not as bad as I thought it would be." But you know all the while it is the worst pain you've ever felt. Sometimes pretending works, for a while.

Sometimes you distract yourself. You focus on other things. Things that are completely irrelevant to the pain you are feeling. Things that may or may not help you keep moving forward, but things that take your mind off the pain. Sometimes these distractions are necessary.

It can be dangerous to acknowledge the pain. To admit it's there. Risky to say out loud, "This hurts, bad! I'm not doing well at all." The risk is you might get stuck there, just letting that voice repeat those words in your head. "This hurts, bad. I'm not doing well at all. I want to quit." The danger is in not ever moving past those words to words more focused on movement, on better things — things yet to come.

It's risky to acknowledge the pain, but sometimes you have to admit it's there.

You may begin talking about the pain matter-of-factly, describing the pain as something that is happening to someone other than you.

Sometimes you need someone right there next to you, encouraging you, reminding you the pain won't last forever. That it will pass. Sometimes you need to be left alone.

When it comes, and sooner or later it will come, you will need to manage it. It will try to take over everything. Your thoughts. Your emotions. Your movement. It will try to stop you dead in your tracks and keep you from the purpose for which you were created, the end to which your life is the means. The pain can consume your every thought if you let it. Don't let it. Acknowledge it. Deal with it. Manage it. And keep going.

It's only fair to warn you, though, that the pain will come. If you have yet to feel it, don't be deluded into thinking you never will. The pain will come, be sure it will come. When it does, all the preparation in the world will fall short of fully preparing you to deal with it. Only experiencing the pain will prepare you for all the times still to come when you will feel it again and again. And each time it comes, you will be a little better at managing the pain than you were the last time you felt it. You will try your best to avoid it, to forget it, to live with it. And, Lord willing, you will keep moving forward.

Relentless Love

"Never be afraid to trust an unknown future to a known God."

CORRIE TEN BOOM

David was not managing the pain of losing Dad well at all. He had spent the eight years since battling his weight, depression, and alcoholism. His weight would fluctuate between 220 pounds and well over 400. As a house painter, he was in and out of work, and his drinking seemed to ebb and flow with his employment. During the previous two years, his situation worsened. He rarely left the basement bedroom at my mom's house.

One day my mom called me frightened and helpless. She told me how David had shaken his son, Tre, in a drunken rage. I didn't know what to do, but I knew I had to do something.

I sat on our couch and wrote him a letter. A love letter. A tough-love letter. I wrote it by hand because there was a blizzard outside, and I would have no way to print it if I typed it on my computer. I needed to write it now and mail it right then, before I changed my mind.

So I wrote several pages about my worry, fear, love, and frustration. I was scared that if something didn't change, I wrote, he wouldn't live long enough to see his kids grow up. And, if he did live long in this state, they might not want to have anything to do with him. David and I talked nearly every day on the phone. In the letter, I told him not to call me until he was ready to talk about what was in it.

Months passed. No calls from David. I began to wonder if we would ever speak again.

Then one day while on the phone with my mom, I heard him in the background.

"Is that Michael? Can I talk to him?"

It had taken him a few months to think about what to say. But something had changed. He knew I loved him. He knew I wasn't trying to judge him but that I missed him, the *him* I knew he could be. The *him* I had always looked up to. He missed that person too. He was ready to try.

During the months that followed, we talked nearly every day again. David still struggled with his weight and depression. He still drank too much, too often. But something was different, something between us. I realized I needed grace as much as he did. That I was no more or less in need of forgiveness. No better, no worse. I was a mess too. David could tell I loved him. And he slowly began to believe God still loved him too.

It was tough to know which was the more life-threatening battle — his weight, which had topped 400 pounds, or his drinking. They were intimately tied to one another.

The tough thing about addiction is it takes so long for a person to admit they need help, that they have a problem they can't solve on their own, that they want help. And when they finally do say it out loud, if they don't have enough money to pay for that help, if they are an out-of-work house painter, then they get added to a three-month waiting list for the public rehab facility. Three months of waiting. Three months to think about backing out. Three months to convince themselves they can't do it. Three months too long.

David had once told our mom, "It's not that I don't believe God can forgive me. It's that I don't think He should."

He felt unforgivable. Unlovable.

When the phone call finally came, it didn't completely surprise me. It didn't come in the middle of the night this time but in the middle of an ordinary day. My mom was sobbing and couldn't get all the words out right. Tre had walked into the basement bedroom where David spent most of his time and found him lying there.

Not moving. Not breathing.

Not again.

Not fair.

Part Two: Between One Loss and Another

Dark Places

"If you want to kiss the sky, better learn how to kneel. On your knees, boy."

U2

It was the first time in years I burst into tears on a training run. I had long since caved to my no music on runs rule. Six years after I signed up for my first marathon. Six years after God first met me on a lonely road while I trudged along, barely running and realizing this running thing was about more than me not getting fat. Six years after I learned God could use running to heal my soul. Six years of marathons and Ironman triathlons and helping start Team World Vision and spending time with the poorest of the poor. Six years of living my dreams. And six months since getting another phone call that changed my life, again.

Here I was, running down North Avenue towards the Chicago lakefront, U2's "Mysterious Ways" blasting through my headphones, tears streaming down my cheeks, crushing a ten-mile tempo run, sobbing uncontrollably, crying so hard I could barely breathe, and running all the harder because of it. I missed them both so much.

Emotional triggers are curious things. Like the words of "Mysterious Ways," the smell of cigarette smoke on a person in the grocery store can bring me to tears. It triggers all of these emotions that seem uncontrollable. It makes me miss my brother David. That smell.

Not the smell of smoke moving through the air, pouring off the end of a lit cigarette. No. I'm talking about the cigarette smoke smell that has settled into a person's everything. Their clothes. Their hair. Their skin. Maybe even their soul. The kind you smell when you hug the person you love that has tried to hide their smoking habit for years because they think you'd disapprove, or judge them, or they are simply embarrassed because they know the habit has left this stink on them. And like the guilt they feel, the smell won't go away.

When I smell that cigarette smell on someone, it makes me want a hug from my big brother David. And because I know that's not possible, that I'll never again get a stinky, cigarette smelling hug from him, it reminds me that part of me is still broken. That pain I feel is excruciating when I think of him slowly becoming a shadow of himself in that dark basement, facing everyday feeling alone and ashamed. Hopeless.

What does God expect from us in dealing with people living in pain and hopelessness? I believe He expects us to pursue them with an unrelenting love, the kind of love with which He pursues us. He expects us to enter into the dark places in which they feel trapped and love them, day after day, week after week, year after year. To let them know we will never leave their side and help them begin to believe there is a hope beyond hope, that life can be worth living and God has a plan for each one of our lives.

What is most often missing in the lives of people living in deep despair is this unrelenting love. They may feel unlovable and need us to prove them wrong. They may feel worthless and need us to make them believe they are valuable to the One who made them. They may feel trapped and need us to show them the light at the end of the tunnel. But rarely do they need us to point out their faults, their sins, their demons. Believe me, they are usually well aware of the things that are self-destructive in their lives. It is often because they don't believe in their own value that they continue in self-destruction. In fact, it is often because we don't believe in our own value that we continue in our own self-destruction.

To go into the dark places where the hopeless spend their lives can be tiring. But we should never grow weary in our efforts to love others. No, we should go into those places and pursue people with the same unrelenting love with which God our Father pursues us. It is only when we truly realize our own depravity in comparison to God's perfect standard that we can understand how desperately we need His grace. It is then that we can see ourselves not as better than those who struggle in hopelessness, but rather on level ground with them. Then our hearts will break for them in such a way that it will motivate us to love them unconditionally, because we know the love God has so freely given to us.

What if each hurting person in this world had not one or two, but ten or twenty people pursuing them with an unrelenting love? Imagine the impact.

I wonder what my brother's life might have been like had he been surrounded by people willing to go into the dark places with him, and love him out. I wonder what might have been if I had been more willing to go there with him, more often. I love you, David. I miss you every day.

Part Three
After

Therapy

"I would rather walk with a friend in the dark, than alone in the light."

HELEN KELLER

After losing David in April 2009, I knew I needed therapy, so I decided to sign up for the Chicago Marathon again.

In the three years since we had started Team World Vision, I had never actually run the marathon with the team. I was always working the event, making sure it was an incredible experience for our runners.

I told the rest of the Team World Vision staff I wanted to run this year. I needed to.

That summer I trained with the Team World Vision Chicago Lakefront training group. The eight runners in my pace group became my therapists.

God used training for my first marathon to heal a lot of hurt in my life as I ran solo, just Him and me. He used this marathon with the team to heal me again, this time running in community, with people who would become lifelong friends.

I always say Team World Vision changes people's lives in Africa and right here in America. I know this to be true from personal experience on both counts.

Love-Hate Relationship

"No road is long with good company."

TURKISH PROVERB

You'd think after all these years, we'd be completely in love all the time. That after all the time we've spent together, all that we've been through, we would never fight. Never get on each other's nerves. Never feel like giving up on each other.

You'd think that because I feel love sometimes, I'd always feel it. But I don't. Sometimes I don't feel very loving. I feel selfish. I want to do what I want to do. I want to do my own thing. Do whatever I feel like.

I can't always be the person I want to be. It's not that easy. There are so many things competing for my attention, so many things that distract me. Sometimes it just feels like work. Hard work.

It's true, I don't always love running. Sometimes I hate it. And I doubt running always loves me. We have a love-hate relationship.

When I got married, a close friend told me love is a choice; you don't always have to feel love to show love. I guess that's how it is when you're a runner. You don't have to feel love for running all the time. You do it because you have made a conscious choice to love it. To love it for the way it makes you feel. To love it for all the good things it has brought into your life. To love it because without it, you wouldn't be the person you are.

Sure I've had to make sacrifices, and on more than one occasion, they have left me feeling disappointed, let down. But more often than not, I've gotten more from running than it's ever gotten from me. If running had the chance, it might even say, "Hey pal, you're not that fun to be around all the time either."

1,000 Rock Stars

"It always seems impossible, until it's done."

NELSON MANDELA

In 2009, less than four years after we launched the pilot of Team World Vision in Chicago, we had 1,000 people toeing the starting line of the Chicago Marathon rocking the orange and blue Team World Vision jerseys. We had become the largest team at one of the biggest marathons in the world.

Of those 1,000 people running the marathon on our team, less than 20 percent had ever run a marathon. Most had never even run a 5K race. They joined the team to make a difference in the lives of children and communities in Africa. When they signed up, they were scared. They had no idea what they were getting themselves into. They had listened to the quiet whisper telling them they had to do this. Just like the whisper I had heard six years earlier when my friend Mark Smith called to tell me he was running the marathon.

That weekend I received the news that World Vision had given the green light for us to make Team World Vision a national program. I immediately hired two of the people who had already been giving me so much of their time, Kirsten Stearns and Lauren Wilgus. Finally, Team World Vision had a staff of more than one. I didn't know then that in just a few years Team World Vision would grow to twenty staff members and hundreds of volunteer coaches, team captains, church teams, corporate teams, and groups of friends all running to help bring clean water to communities in Africa. I had no idea we would get to help launch Team World Vision in other countries. At the time, I was just thrilled that we had a team, and soaking in the feel of 1,000 teammates sharing the dream to help change the world.

One thousand rock stars.

Tougher

"If you're feeling helpless, help someone."

AUNG AAN SUU KYI

I was twenty-five when my dad died. When David died, he left four kids — David, eight, Maddie, ten, Bailey, twelve, and Tre, sixteen. His wife, my sister-in-law Jamie, was my age, a widow at thirty-four. My mom says losing David was tougher than losing Dad. Sometimes I think she has forgotten how tough it was to lose Dad. Sometimes I agree with her.

I believe this much is true. As tough as it was on me, it was much harder on David to lose our dad. And it was much harder for my nieces and nephews to lose their dad at eight, ten, twelve, and sixteen, than it was for me to lose my dad when I was 25.

I realize these are difficult and perhaps pointless arguments to make. Was it tougher for my mom to lose my dad after thirty-five years of marriage than it was for her mother to lose my Grandpa Mills after sixty-five years together? Is it easier to lose a family member to cancer because at least you can say goodbye? Is it more painful for a mother to lose her daughter to a preventable disease because they have no access to an immunization shot that costs fifty cents than for a mother whose son is hit by a car?

Pain is relative, and it's a distraction. If we spend too much time concerned with our own pain, we forget to tend to the pain of others. Our own pain too often forces us inward when the thing that will help us heal most is to turn our attention toward relieving the pain of others. No matter how deep our hurt, there is someone with a deeper pain. Rather than sit in our own despair, we should set out to do something to relieve theirs. People experience pain that is far beyond what we can even imagine.

Comrades

> *"Never underestimate the power of a few committed people to change the world. Indeed, it is the only thing that ever has."*
>
> MARGARET MEADE

Josh Cox had been telling me for months about the Comrades Marathon, the oldest and largest ultramarathon in the world. Twenty-thousand people were expected to run the fifty-six mile race that year. The course is notorious for its relentless ups and downs and winding hills. Runners must complete the entire course within twelve hours or they are disqualified from the race.

Josh holds the American record in the 50K (31 miles). He was hoping to be the first American in decades to win the race. And I had no interest in running the same race and finishing dead last. So I told him straight out, no, I would not run Comrades with him. Not now. Not ever.

Three months later, I had changed my tune. Josh and I were hanging out at a post-race Power Bar party following the New York City Marathon with Andy Baldwin, a U.S. Naval doctor and contestant on The Bachelor, Season 10. Josh got Andy to agree to run it for Team World Vision, but Andy said, "I'll do it if Chitwood does it." To which I replied, "I'll do it if we can get 1,000 kids sponsored."

In the days that followed, I made a list of my top twenty people to ask. I figured in order to get ten, I'd have to ask twenty.

One of the people on my list was Steve Spear, a campus pastor for Willow Creek Community Church.

"Paul JVR is in." I told him, knowing this would up the ante. (Paul's last name is Jansen Van Rensburg so everyone calls him JVR for short.) In 2008, Steve and JVR had been the first pastors to put a church team together for Team World Vision at the Chicago Marathon. They had since helped raise hundreds of thousands of dollars for clean water through Team World Vision. JVR had grown up in South Africa and had wanted to run Comrades since he was a kid.

"What?" Steve responded with surprise.

"Yep. He committed the first time I called him. He's in. He didn't even hesitate. We need you, bro. It's going to be awesome."

I knew telling Steve that Paul JVR was in might tip him toward running with us. Get JVR first, then get Steve. That was my plan.

Thinking I was calling to thank him for being an inaugural supporter of Team World Vision with his church, Steve said, "Chitwood, you've got a funny way of thanking people. I thought you were going to invite me out to a nice dinner."

"Steve, other than fear, what is holding you back?" I asked.

"Michael, it's definitely fear that's holding me back. It's all kinds of fear," he said.

Just about every great thing God has for us in this life lies on the other side of fear. And it requires that we walk through fear to get to it. The thing about fear is, it's scary. We want guarantees. We want to eliminate all risks of failure before trying something. We want to know how it's going to turn out before we commit. We delude ourselves in thinking this is possible. Faith requires taking steps into the unknown. It requires that we trust that trying and failing is more valuable than not trying at all. It requires that we believe a life worth living is one full of adventure. Full of failing, but full of trying.

"Steve," I told him, "take another day and pray about this." The next day he said yes.

A dream team followed. A bunch of my closest friends agreed to run it with us, and a few new ones.

Part Three: After

The Dream Team

"You don't get to choose when opportunity is going to knock, so you better be prepared for it when it does."
TED ANDERSON

"How in the world is he going to run Comrades in four weeks?" I thought while watching Bart Yasso struggle to run three miles.

Bart is known as "The Mayor of Running" and is the Chief Running Officer at *Runner's World* magazine. He has run races on every continent and has taken on some of the most challenging races in the world. That was before disease took hold of his body.

Bart is battling Lyme Disease, which has left him with a limp in one leg and chronic severe pain. We were four weeks out from Comrades, the one race Bart never checked off his bucket list, the one race, as he had said for years, still haunted his dreams. I watched as he struggled to maintain a twelve-minute pace for a short three-mile run. After the run he told me, "That was the hardest run of my life," and I believed him.

I had to ask, "Bart, how are you going to do Comrades in four weeks?" His response: "I'm going to will myself to the finish line."

Andy Baldwin called me a month out from the race, "Chitwood, I think I broke my leg."

"What? Andy, you're a doctor. What do you mean you *think* you broke your leg?"

He was going in for a bone scan that day. He was nervous. Andy wasn't usually the kind of guy to ask someone to pray for him, but he did that day. I prayed with him and tried give him some encouragement.

The bone scan was inconclusive, and he was told not to run for six weeks. The race was in four. He didn't run a step from then until race day.

When he met me at the hotel in Durban, South Africa, two days before Comrades, I could see it on his face. He was scared.

"Chitwood, I'm going to do it. I'm going to go out there and try to run this thing. But I'm scared. My leg might be broken. If it is, it could really give out on me. It could break clean through. I'm gonna give it my best."

Andy is a doctor in the U.S. Navy. Apparently they teach you to be a tough guy in the Navy, because this dude is tough. He was scared, and I was scared for him.

Paul Martin, one of three Pauls on our Comrades team, ran backward on the downhill sections. It was easier for him to hit stride running backward on his prosthetic leg. Paul lost his leg about five inches below the knee in an accident that involved a drunk driver. Sadly, Paul was the drunk driver. Mercifully, no one was killed.

After the accident, Paul realized his life had been out of control. Instead of lying down and giving up, he started taking up sports, one after the other. He has been on the U.S. disabled alpine ski team, U.S. Paralympic hockey and cycling teams, U.S. Olympic Committee's Disabled Athlete of the Year, and the Ironman leg amputee world record holder.

When he signed up for our team, he was pretty sure he could cover the distance but was worried about the hills and the friction it would cause on "Stumpy," the nickname he gave to the place where his leg was amputated. Paul would need to stop every four or five miles to take his prosthetic leg off and pour out the sweat.

I can't imagine how other runners at Comrades must have felt being passed at mile fifty by a guy with one leg running backward downhill.

The day of Comrades, I ran my best race ever. But for Josh Cox, it was a different story.

Granted, my perfect day meant I finished in just over nine hours, and Josh's horrible day still brought him across the finish line in less than seven and a half. But, he was hoping to win. He had trained to win. He knew he could win.

Something went wrong, it went wrong early, and it never got better. Stomach issues. The kind that leave you in the bathroom for a while. That is, if there were a bathroom around. In an ultra, there is typically not a bathroom when you need one, so the side of the road has to do.

His stomach issues left him completely dehydrated within the first fifteen miles. By mile twenty, he knew he was in trouble. Big trouble.

Things like this happen. Pro runners have bad races. The smart thing for Josh to do was to pull out of the race. With this kind of dehydration, this early in the race, he risked doing some serious damage to his body. His calves had cramped bad, worse than they ever had before. He probably should have pulled out of the race and saved his legs for another day. A day when he could capitalize on the months of training he had put in. Finishing this race would just tear his body down, and he even risked serious injury. It would definitely mean he wouldn't be able to race again for a while. A long while. He risked permanent damage to his legs if he continued.

The only problem with the thought of quitting was a little

South African girl named Phillile, Josh's World Vision sponsored child. Phillile had come to watch Josh run. The World Vision South Africa staff had been telling her for weeks about her sponsor coming to meet her. How he was a famous American runner. How he was coming to compete at Comrades, the biggest race in South Africa. She had seen his picture on the cover of the newspapers. She had waited for weeks to watch him. She would be at the finish line, waiting for him.

Against all better judgment, Josh decided he couldn't let her down.

It took some serious humility and courage for Josh to keep moving forward that day. He holds the American record in the 50K, has run in four U.S. Olympic Marathon trials, and typically wins or places near the top of every race he runs. But this day, his body had failed him so badly, he found himself standing on the side of the road long enough to let hundreds, maybe thousands of runners pass him.

"Hey, are you Josh Cox?" a runner would say. "What are you doing back here with us?"

Sure, it would've been easier to just call it a day. Save the legs, and race again soon. Make the smart decision. Pro marathoners only get to race a couple of times a year. By running through this, he was basically wasting months of training and risking long-term injury.

"You're my girl. You're my girl. You know what. You're the one. You are why I finished," Josh told Phillile after crossing the finish line of Comrades.

After the race Josh shared his heart.

"To have a race not go as planned. To have your

hopes and goals and dreams set for a fifty-six-mile race. And to think for two seconds that's what this is about is totally wrong. This is about so much more. And I just thank God for the opportunity to come over here and race, and to meet Phillile. Not only having her there at the finish, but she's what kept me going during the race. Then to come here and meet her family and walk her home from school. This is more than I could have ever hoped for or imagined. Just absolutely amazing."

After Josh, Todd Katter crossed the finish line, then a few minutes later, Hannah Covert, then Rusty Funk, then me. That meant I got to watch the rest of the team come in. Andy Baldwin made it in. No broken leg. Smiling. One by one they came, and we were right there to cheer them in: Kendall, JVR, Martin and Travis, then Tony, Paul Courtney, Steve Spear, Paul Martin (who took off his prosthetic leg and hopped over the finish line on one foot), Scott, and Laura.

We were all there. Almost. All but two were finished, Bart and Thad. With just thirty minutes to go, we were getting worried. At Comrades you have twelve hours to complete the race; then they fire a gun, and a line of men lock arms at the finish line. No more runners are allowed to cross. That's it. A runner might be ten feet from the finish line, twelve hours and five seconds, and they are not allowed to finish. It would be as if they were never even there. We were concerned to say the least.

Finally with twenty minutes to spare, we saw Bart make the final turn. He had made it. He had certainly seen better days, but this dude had literally willed himself to the finish line despite his body protesting for nearly twelve hours his decision to run Comrades.

Fifteen minutes to go and still no sign of Thad. We were able to check his splits and see that with an hour left in the race, he had been just four miles from the finish line. That meant he only had to average fifteen minutes per mile to make the cut-off. But from the looks of some of the runners coming across the line that late in the race, it was very possible he was moving slower than that. Each of our seventeen Team World Vision finishers was waiting with our hearts in our stomachs. Waiting for Thad, waiting for our team to be complete for our victory celebration.

When we saw him enter the stadium with just a little more than ten minutes to spare, we lost it. We had gotten all eighteen of our team members across the finish line of one of the toughest races in the world. A 100 percent finisher rate for Team World Vision's first international team, first ultra, first Comrades.

That night, back at our hotel, we sat around a large dining room table eating our fill. Paul Martin, along with every one of our Team World Vision runners, had just completed the Ultimate Human Race. But only Paul had done it on a prosthetic leg.

Paul stood up and told us there had been only one other occasion where he shared this special honor with anyone. We would be among a select group of people to partake in this special symbol of our team, our family.

He then proceeded to fill up his prosthetic leg with beer and passed it down the table to each person, and each one of us took a drink from Paul Martin's leg. The one that had just carried him fifty-six miles through the hills of South Africa. The one he had taken off every few miles to empty the sweat out of. He assured us it had been thoroughly cleaned.

Josh spent the day after Comrades with Phillile. He visited her home, where her grandparents told him he and his wife, Carrie, had brought hope to Phillile. Since her parents died, Phillile's grandparents said she had been very quiet. But hearing about her new sponsors, her new family across the ocean, had given her a renewed spirit. As she hugged Josh, I heard her whisper to him, "I love you." Josh held her and whispered back, "I love you too, Phillile."

When Josh and Andy talked me into running Comrades with them, we asked a total of 20 people to run it with us. Ultimately, eighteen said yes and two said no.

The two who said no, I'm sure they had their reasons. It cost too much. They didn't have the time to train. They were nervous about asking people to sponsor a child. They couldn't ask for the time off from work. Maybe they doubted it would be worth the sacrifices required. Fear won.

I wish I could tell you they regretted their decision not to take on this challenge with us; that they deeply regret staying home while the rest of us had the adventure of our lives. The truth is they have no idea what they missed. They can't even begin to understand the incredible, life-changing experience Comrades was for every single one of us. They will just go on with their life as though nothing even happened, as though they didn't say no to the opportunity to live life to its fullest, the chance to help change the lives of a thousand children in Africa.

We all miss it sometimes. Opportunity. The whisper comes to us, inviting us to something that requires sacrifice or risk or work, it requires stepping through fear, and adjusting plans, it requires that we leave our comfort zone. So, far too often, we let it pass us by. We miss it, and we don't even realize what it is that we've missed.

The Best View in the World

"If you want to go fast, go alone. If you want to go far, go together."

AFRICAN PROVERB

My favorite view in the world is from the top of a mountain in Marich Pass, Kenya. From this mountaintop, you can see for miles. The climb up the mountain is long and tough, but that view is worth it. Across the Great Rift Valley, little villages of thatch-roofed mud homes as far as you can see. Mountains and hills and valleys. This is the home of the world's greatest distance runners.

It's not only the natural beauty of God's creation that makes this my favorite view in the world. It's the brainchild of David Kingo that has me mesmerized.

David is the Kenyan water engineer that designed the fifty-mile pipeline that runs up and down the mountainside, defying gravity as the water runs uphill. The spider web of steel pipe starts high in the mountains, where a river meets a dam. The water flows through miles of steel pipe, fifty miles by the time it reaches the people. It goes through a treatment system and into five large water tanks that lie miles apart atop other smaller mountains. From there, the water runs through smaller pipes to every edge of the vista. The water project is so impressive that pictures don't begin to do it justice.

To put it in perspective, a typical well in a rural African community provides water to about four hundred people. This pipeline brings water to nearly 100,000. World Vision's engineers know water is not a one-size-fits-all issue. They use a variety of solutions depending on the context. Pipelines, borehole wells, rock catchments, rainwater harvesting, dams, capped springs, and water treatments are just a few of the solutions that can be implemented. But behind this hardware is years of software that is built in a community by World Vision staff.

Capacity-building and empowerment are a huge part of what makes these projects sustainable: educating community members about basic germ theory, hygiene, and sanitation, like washing your hands and not going to the bathroom near your drinking water source; training local people to maintain and repair broken wells; creating a Water Users Association and Committee to collect fees that will ensure sustainability and independence, so the project will last long after World Vision leaves. This is all part of the transformational community development model. This is the part that amazes me even more than a fifty-mile pipeline.

Andy Baldwin was serving for one month at a mission medical clinic in Kenya when he bumped into some government water engineers. He told them he had visited a water project the previous year with World Vision. "Which one?" they asked. "The one in Marich Pass," he told them.

They said they knew it well. "We all told David Kingo it could not be done. There was no way to get those pipes up that mountain. We couldn't believe that they accomplished it."

What those engineers hadn't taken into account was the strength that comes from a community when it works together. When people refuse to listen to the word "can't."

How had they gotten those pipes up the mountain, pipes that weigh 1,200 pounds each? How did they get those pipes up a mountain with terrain so rough trucks could not make the climb?

The men from the villages had done it together. Fifteen men per pipe, they carried fifty miles of pipe up that mountain, one section at a time.

It's those men and their commitment to their community that makes this my favorite view in the world.

On top of a mountain in Kenya, I can watch the sun rise and set on the most beautiful landscape in the world. I can see the beauty of God's creation in a way few people will ever experience. From that mountaintop, looking out over the villages below, I can see the best of humanity.

Maurine

"The King will reply, 'Truly I tell you, whatever you did for one of the least of these brothers and sisters of mine, you did for me.'"

MATTHEW 25:40

She started screaming and crying her eyes out the second I handed it to her. She had no clue what it was, who I was, or why I looked so strange.

I was the first *mzungu* Maurine had ever met, the first white person. She was three years old. We sat in her thatch-roof mud home with her mother, Josphine, and her five siblings. As if my strange white skin wasn't enough to frighten this poor little girl, she thought the stuffed animal I gave her as a present was an actual dead animal. "What kind of crazy man is this?" she must have been thinking.

She owned my heart from the first moment I saw her. She sat on a blue wooden bench with three boys who all looked to be a year or two older than her, her bare dusty feet dangling a foot off the ground.

The first Americans to ever visit this community deep in the mountains of the Baringo District in Bartabwa, Kenya, we stood waiting to meet our World Vision sponsored children.

World Vision's program is the world's largest child sponsorship program with over four million kids sponsored around the world.

But it is unique from other programs in so many ways. If World Vision simply took my $35 per month and gave it to Maurine's mother, it could not provide clean water to drink. It could not give her a school to go to, or a health clinic for when she gets sick.

World Vision focuses on helping children through community development. If you combine my $35 per month with the $35 per month of a thousand other people who sponsor children in Maurine's community, now we're talking some serious impact. This is how World Vision is able to tackle massive projects and initiatives, like providing clean water to 50,000 people in an area, building schools and the bridges needed to access them, building dams to provide irrigation canals to 1,000 farmers in an area.

When I met Maurine for the first time, she and her family had no access to safe water. In fact her mother, Josphine, had to walk two miles down the mountain, several times a day, to carry water home that wasn't even safe to drink. Child mortality in her community was fifty percent. At three years old, Maurine had already outlived many of her friends.

It's the very water she drinks that could kill her. And it's the clean water project that was being completed that would keep her and countless others alive for generations to come.

The last time I visited Maurine, the ground had been broken. Solar-powered pumps were bringing water to huge water tanks, earthen dams helped create water pans that formed giant lakes for water to be piped from, natural springs had been capped, and storage tanks and water spigots were installed. The World Vision engineers had taken a comprehensive approach to solving the water problem in Bartabwa. It wasn't easy, but they were taking a community that had virtually no access to safe water and transforming it.

I'm spoiled rotten that I've had the chance to spend time with Maurine and her family on several occasions. She no longer cries when she sees me but runs to me with her arms wide open. Her mother knows me and welcomes me as part of her family. Her siblings smile and practice their English with me. Maurine is the poorest friend I have in the world, and she has enriched my life beyond measure.

Worn-Out Shoes

"Don't judge a man until you've walked a mile in his shoes."

UNKNOWN

It was my favorite day with my brother David since losing Dad. Almost exactly a year after I wrote the letter to him, begging him to get help, I drove from Chicago to Grand Rapids to spend the entire day with him. He was finally ready to try getting the help he needed.

We met at a Panera for lunch. I sensed a hope in him that had been missing for nearly a decade since losing Dad. We talked about how his biggest dreams were all for his kids.

"I don't dream about making a lot of money, or having some dream job," he told me. "I just want to be able to provide for Jamie and my kids." He really wanted to be able to take them on a vacation too. Nothing big, just a trip to Cedar Point or Sea World.

I realized my dreams for David were so different from his. Maybe because my vision for his life was so big, maybe because he had given up hope for his own life and only dreamed for his kids now. Or maybe it was because his love for his kids was so deep. I wanted to see him using his gifts working with people with disabilities. It was so hard watching him go in and out of work as a house painter. I could see the glimmer of hope in him through the fear in his eyes that he might fail.

I struggled to know how to help. David was willing to work

hard, and proved it by taking any job he could get. One job had him sandblasting the underground pipes at a water treatment plant, standing in stinking sewage all day shoveling sludge. He never complained about working. When he could find work, he worked twelve-hour days doing hard labor. But his confidence was low. He was so big he could hardly even get painters clothes that fit him. He was willing to do any job but had a hard time getting one.

Maurine and Josphine in Kenya are the poorest friends I have in the world. But my brother David was an intimate reminder of how rich I actually am. David and I wore the same size shoe, so I would give him my running shoes when they had too many miles on them. He could never believe I would stop wearing shoes that didn't seem worn out. I had a car with insurance, and so did my wife. I had a paycheck I could count on every two weeks. I had health insurance. I had clothes that weren't stained with paint, and shoes with no holes in them. This and the fact that I knew I had to find a way to insist on paying for lunch and the movie without making him feel inadequate for not being able to afford treating his little brother to lunch.

David wanted to lose the weight, but it was tough to even know where to start. With his reconstructed ankle and at his weight, he couldn't walk, much less run for exercise. My friend Tommy helped me get him a decent stationary bike, which he tried to use. But he was too embarrassed to use it around his family. He put it in the basement of my mom's house and only used it when no one was around.

He wanted to get help with his drinking, but with no insurance and no money, he was put on a waiting list for a public rehab program and waited.

In the months that followed, David's resolve to go to rehab

ebbed and flowed. Several times he would go a week or two or even a month without a drink, convincing himself maybe he could do it on his own, without help.

His fear of going into a rehab facility came to a head on a trip to Texas for a week-long painting job a friend had got him. Seth had been an alcoholic and beaten his addiction. Since the rehab facility was taking so long to admit David, Seth had talked him into coming to Texas for a week to do a job, hoping he could help keep the demons at bay until the facility had a bed for David. The trip had the opposite effect.

Seth was a huge encouragement to David the entire time, but it was on that trip that David became acutely aware of how embarrassing it would be to share a room with another person. He had always been a terrible snorer when he slept, but now at nearly 400 pounds, it had gotten much worse. He was starting to get cold feet about the rehab program. But he wasn't backing out.

We ate and talked for a few hours. Then we went to see a movie, *Eagle Eye*. It's the last movie I ever saw with my brother.

What I remember most from that day was laughing with him. I hadn't seen him laugh so hard in too many years.

On the drive home to Chicago, I thought about how much fun it was to spend time with David, how much I loved having him as a close friend, and how much he needed me. I decided to take one day a month off from work to drive to Michigan to spend a day with him. I had hoped to help him find a way to lose the weight. We even had started talking about him training for a fifty-mile bike ride with me, and I was looking for a bike for him. I had hoped to see him get into rehab and beat alcohol once and for all. None of this ever happened. The hope he found was too little. The help he sought came too late.

A few months after he died, while I was training for the Chicago Marathon with my Team World Vision therapy group, my shoes hit their mileage limit. My first thought was to send them to David. A few years have passed now, but a pair of running shoes with too many miles on them can still make me cry.

The Amish Are On to Something

"It's the greatest poverty to decide that a child must die so that you may live as you wish."

MOTHER TERESA

While we are living in excess and extravagance, people are dying because they don't have enough food to eat or safe water to drink. The reality is people are dying because we aren't sharing what God gave us. The money and resources we have don't belong to us but rather are entrusted to us.

Some people say, "How can God let people starve to death or let children die because they don't have safe water to drink? How can a loving God allow kids to die of things like diarrhea or malaria?"

The truth is, God could ask us the same question. How could we let these things happen? He has trusted us with all the resources to meet these needs. Often we wait around hoping governments or rich people will solve these problems. By global standards, we are the rich people.

The first time my friend Princess came to the U.S. she cried when she ate her first meal. It was enough to feed her whole family back home. Living simply is tough when we are constantly bombarded with messages that tell us we have to have whatever is being sold to us that day. Things we are made to think we cannot live without. But we can live without most of them. And if we choose to live without some of the stuff we don't need, we can help others live life to its fullest.

Lauren, a friend of mine, and her sister, Emily, decided to give up cable so they could sponsor a kid through World Vision. This says something about their priorities and finances. First, it says they think a child's life is more important than what's on TV. It also tells me that if they had to give up cable so they could afford $35 per month, they don't really have much wiggle room in their budget. They actually had to give something up to help someone else. They had to make a choice in their priorities. They asked, "What's more important to me, the life of a child or *The Real Housewives* of whatever city the real housewives are from this season?"

A friend once told me excess is having more than we need when others don't have enough to meet their basic needs. The truth is that all things come at a cost. The stuff we spend our money on can cost other people their very lives. At the end of the movie *Schindler's List*, Oskar Schindler, who had been buying freedom for Jews out of Nazi captivity, begins looking at all of his material possessions. Then he looks down at his wristwatch and begins to calculate how much more money could he have gotten and how many lives could he have saved if only he weren't so attached to his stuff.

God's Pleasure

"For it is God who is producing in you both the desire and the ability to do what pleases Him."

PHILLIPIANS 2:13

The *Chariots of Fire* theme song is the only song I sort of remember how to play on the piano. I wasted my parents' money for three years by not practicing before they let me quit piano lessons. The movie made little impact on me as a kid except for that song that has come to be synonymous with running.

In the movie, Olympic runner Eric Liddell is defending his desire to run to his sister Jennie. He had just missed a prayer meeting because he was running. Jennie wanted Eric to give up his dreams of being a runner.

His reply: "I believe that God made me for a purpose. But He also made me fast, and when I run, I feel His pleasure."

I was with some friends from our Team World Vision staff, waiting for a table at a restaurant. My friend John Huddle had recently watched *Chariots of Fire* and, inspired by Liddell, he asked, "Michael, when do you feel God's pleasure?'

I was dumbfounded, stunned. I stood there in silence for some time. I racked my brain for an answer, something that would pass for truth. But John is one of those rare people that can see right through you and into your soul. I couldn't lie. I didn't have an answer.

"When do I feel God's pleasure? You know, John, I guess not

that often."

He must have been able to tell his question cut deep. He let it go.

I didn't. I wrestled with that question for weeks. I had told John the truth. I didn't feel God's pleasure often. I sometimes felt His presence. Occasionally I felt His comfort. But His pleasure? I wasn't even sure I knew what it meant.

While the previous ten years of my life had brought some amazing experiences, they held more pain and heartache than I ever knew possible. It was a question that didn't make sense in my spirit.

When did I feel God's pleasure? In the weeks after John asked it, a different question kept coming to my mind: "Why should *I* get to feel God's pleasure?"

At that same time John asked me this question, there was a severe famine in the Horn of Africa. I knew at that very moment there was a mother walking from Somalia to Kenya day and night, walking with her children. Walking tirelessly hoping to find help in the refugee camps. All the time not knowing there would be no room left in the camps by the time she got there. Not knowing that two of her children would not survive the journey. Not knowing she had only begun to experience the depth of pain this life had to deal out for her; that there was more to come, hell on earth.

When did *she* get to feel God's pleasure?

What would ever make me feel I had the right to?

A few weeks after he asked the question, I still couldn't stop thinking about it.

Finally, I gave John the best answer I could find:

"John, there's a little girl in a small village in Kenya. Her name is Maurine, and she was three the first time I met her. At first I couldn't tell how Maurine's mom, Josphine, felt about the strange man with the pale skin who was here with her family. She nodded when I asked questions, and I soon realized she understood more English than she could speak. Every so often she would raise her eyebrows and give me a half smile. Since the first time we met, I have visited Maurine, Josphine and their family several times. Each time it feels more like home, like family.

Josphine can't even afford to buy the small piece of dirt on which her thatched-roof mud home sits. She is the poorest friend I have in this world. Her family has needs and fears and worries the likes of which I have never had to know. When her husband left her alone with six children and no way to provide for their most basic needs, she felt hopeless. I wonder if she ever feels God's pleasure when she walks to fetch water each day, two miles each way, three times a day; water that isn't even safe to drink; water that could take Maurine's life. I wonder if she ever feels God's pleasure when she lies awake at night worried there won't be enough food to keep her children healthy or alive. I wonder if she ever feels God's pleasure when the others in her village whisper about why her husband left her. I wonder if she ever feels God's pleasure, ever.

Josphine tells me we were the answer to her prayers. But I know the truth. That she was the answer to mine.

John, that's when I feel God's pleasure, when I'm in Kenya with Maurine and her mother Josphine and her sisters and brothers. While Josphine has been praying for a better life for her kids, for some kind of hope, thousands of people that run with me back home have been asking their friends to give money to help a mother and her children they will never meet. A family that I get to see changed by the love of strangers a world away. And in that moment, I realize that to them, I am no longer a stranger a world away, but I am family, and I am here, with them. I love being there with them. And it's then that I feel God's pleasure."

Family Ride

"What lies behind you and what lies in front of you pales in comparison to what lies inside of you."

RALPH WALDO EMERSON

One day we were sitting together in our old house, the one I grew up in. I think it was our dining room, but I can't remember for sure. My mom was sitting next to me, my brother David was on the other side facing me, and Dad was across from mom. We were just talking. Dan was in the other room. I think he was on the phone or something, because I could hear him talking to someone.

My dad said he made some food for anyone who was doing the ride. I couldn't believe he and my mom were going to do a bike ride together. I was shocked they had trained for it and there was no way I was going to pass this up. Dad had thought ahead in packing a lunch for us, but I wondered if he had packed the right kind of food for an event like this. "How did he know what to pack? He's never done anything like this," I thought to myself.

I wasn't sure what distance they planned to do that day, but I was hoping they were up for at least 50 miles, maybe even 100. Just as I started to tell him I was in for the ride, I realized only David wasn't. There was no way he could do that kind of bike ride. His ankle caused him so much pain, and I was sure he hadn't trained. Even though I didn't live at home anymore, I would have known if he had been training to ride with us. I hesitated to tell Dad I was going to ride with them. I didn't want David to feel left out. I saw his eyes drop a little and his spirit did the same. He didn't want to let us know how our doing this without him hurt. I wondered how often he had felt that way. He didn't want to keep us from doing the ride together. But it was clear he wished he could join us.

One of us, I can't remember who, changed the subject for a minute, and that's when I noticed they had painted the dining room gray. Why did they do that? It made the whole room feel too dark. Was it the paint color or just the mood of the conversation?

When David stood up, something was different about him. Something was so different, but I couldn't put my finger on it at first. I'm not sure how I hadn't noticed, but I think it's because he was sitting down from the moment I saw him. It took my breath away. David must have lost 150 pounds. He looked amazing. He was still a big guy, maybe 250 pounds. But when I hugged him, my arms went all the way around and I felt my hands touch behind him.

David was always proud of me, the weight I lost, the races I did, and especially for helping start Team World Vision. But he never came to a Team World Vision event. In fact, the only race he did come to was a half Ironman I did with Dan. It was in Michigan, just an hour from where we grew up. My mom came and so did David. He brought his wife and kids, and so did Dan, so they could all watch together. The kids got to play on the beach while they waited for us to finish. I remember feeling bad for David that day, like I was leaving him out. That's how I felt this day talking about the bike ride with my parents.

As I hugged David I could hear Dan in the other room, still on the phone I assumed. I heard the kids playing together. They were Dan's kids and David's kids because Dani and I didn't have kids yet. They were playing a little too loudly and I heard someone playing music. I couldn't figure out what instrument the person in the other room was playing, either the piano or a guitar, I thought. Whatever it was, it was distracting.

I couldn't get over how much weight David had lost. Maybe he had been training with Mom and Dad for the ride and they decided to surprise me. He and I had talked so many times about doing a bike ride together. "But why didn't he say he was coming with us? Why did he get so uncomfortable when we were talking about it?" I kept thinking. And, then I thought, "Why is that music getting louder?" It wasn't a guitar, but chimes maybe.

I started to realize maybe we hadn't been sitting in our dining room. It was so gray. There is no way Dad would paint the dining room gray. I'm not sure what room we were sitting in talking, me, my dad, Dan and David, and my mom.

I hugged David again and I had to fight back tears. "Don't cry," I told myself, "Don't let him know you are hurting like this for him. He'll be so embarrassed."

While I was hugging David, I was so proud of him and ashamed of myself for not having been able to help him do this sooner. He must have worked so hard to lose that weight. Why hadn't he told me before now? And Dad, he should have said something to me about it. It wasn't like him to not brag about something like this. Why wasn't he bragging about it?

"It's a harp. Not a guitar. Not a piano. Not chimes. It's a harp. Why is someone playing a harp?" I remember thinking as I hugged David.

Soon after I realized it was a harp, I also started to realize the sound was coming from just a few feet away, not the other room. It was my iPhone. The alarm I had set the night before.

I held tighter to David and the tears started, first with one and then another. I didn't want to get up for work. I wanted to stay here with David, in my dream.

But Rusty was picking me up at 5 AM. We had to get up early and drive to Michigan. Not to visit my dad or David. They aren't there anymore. We never got to have a real conversation about doing a ride together. My dad died before I even ran my first marathon. David never got healthy enough to ride with me. I wasn't going to see my family that day. This was a work trip. I had to talk to some folks about running in races to help kids in Africa. Had to keep moving forward. Stay distracted. Focus on things other than missing Dad and David. But if I could, if I had the chance, I would have stayed there with him, hugging my brother just a while longer.

Close Calls

"Come to Me, all who are weary and heavy-laden, and I will give you rest."

JESUS CHRIST

When I answered the phone my twelve-year-old niece, Bailey, was on the line, crying hysterically.

It took some work to calm her down and get what she was trying to say through her hyperventilating and crying. "Grandma was in a bad car wreck." Her grandma. My mom.

I got the call a few weeks after getting back from South Africa. My mom had come with me to watch me run my second Comrades. It had been an incredible trip. The best time I had had with my mom in the nine years since losing Dad. Our first trip to another country together since the first one we took to Haiti twelve years earlier, just two years before my dad died. She was with me when God wrecked my heart for the poor. It was therapeutic for both of us and it meant the world to me for her to cheer me on from the side of the roads that lead from Durban to Pietermaritzburg.

Even once I got Bailey calmed down, she didn't have much information. Mom had been in a bad car wreck and was at the hospital. She had hit her head pretty bad and had been admitted to the intensive care unit.

By the time I got to talk to her on the phone, she had seen the doctor. The good news, he told her, was there were no broken bones. The bad news, he continued, was her lymph nodes were swollen. The only explanation was cancer.

Cancer? This can't be right. We just spent two weeks in South Africa together. It had been the healthiest I'd seen her in years. I knew the drill. I called my wife to tell her and packed my bag. Twenty minutes later I was in the car making the drive from Chicago to Grand Rapids. The drive was all too familiar as was the heavy heart I carried. Three hours later I was at the hospital with Mom.

When you've watched your dad die in a hospital from a routine shoulder surgery, seeing your mom in a hospital room after being in a car wreck and then being told she has cancer is more than a little disconcerting. The doc told us if she scheduled the proper tests it could take weeks for them to get her in, but if they admitted her to the hospital they could get them done in a matter of days. The idea of waiting weeks for test results was unbearable. Mom checked in.

The doctors had been sure it was cancer. They didn't even consider any other possibilities. They were wrong. It was a lung infection. The treatment would be brutal on mom's body, not all that different from the chemotherapy cancer would have required, but for some reason it was a lot less scary.

Almost losing people who are close to you is a lot tougher when you've actually lost people close to you. Every close call, every near miss, every call you get in the middle of the night, every visit to the hospital, you think to yourself, this could be it. I know what this feels like, and I don't really feel up to this right now. These close calls leave me thinking, "God, I know it's coming back for me, the pain of loss, but please, just not yet."

100 Miles

"Run when you can, walk if you have to, crawl if you must; just never give up."

DEAN KARNAZES

"He needs to go to the hospital, now." I heard the words, but it took me a few minutes to figure out who said them, and who they were talking about.

I was laying face down on the grass. I could barely move, completely exhausted, a mylar blanket over me to keep the chills at bay. My feet felt like they had been smashed with a sledgehammer, every bone broken, every tendon ripped to shreds. It may have looked as though I was going in and out of consciousness, but I was really just resting my eyes. That's what my dad used to tell me when he fell asleep in his La-Z-Boy but didn't want me to change the channel on the TV. I would ask him if he was asleep, my way of saying, "Dad, you're sleeping, let me have the remote. I don't want to watch "Murder She Wrote." He'd lift his eyelids less than halfway, "I'm just resting my eyes."

I was just resting my eyes, but man was I tired. I'd been up for nearly thirty hours.

Someone was calling my name. I didn't recognize the voice but knew his face when I lifted my head off the ground and saw Mac squatting down next to me. Mac is a Team World Vision runner and a former paramedic. He was checking on the four of us, Rusty, Hannah, JVR, and me. The four of us were all in the same condition, or so we thought. We were lying about twenty feet from one another on the ground outside the Team World Vision post-race tent at the Chicago Marathon. Our team had raised close to $1 million for World Vision's clean water projects. Inside the tent were nearly 1,000 of our teammates who had just run the Chicago Marathon. We had run the race with them, only we had decided to tack a few miles on before the start of the race. Seventy-three-point-eight miles to be exact.

"Chitwood!"

I looked up at Mac and made eye contact, then heard him say, "Yeah, Chitwood looks okay."

I realized he was checking each of us to see how we were doing. A few minutes later I heard him say, "Let's get JVR to the hospital, now."

It all started fifteen months earlier, the day before we ran fifty-six miles at the Comrades Marathon in South Africa. Rusty told me it would be his one and only ultramarathon. After this he was sticking with 26.2 miles. Marathons were far enough. The day after we ran Comrades, Rusty told me he wanted to run 100 miles.

Rusty always says, "Don't ever make the mistake of telling Chitwood you want to do something ridiculous. He won't let it go."

I say it was his crazy idea. He just needed a little nudging on it.

That's how it happened with the 100. The day after Comrades, Rusty was a bit *runmotional* as we call it. It's happens during or after a big race, when all the testosterone has been spent, and you begin getting weepy. You feel like a little child. All you want to do is cuddle. Or tell people you love them. Or say stupid things like, "I want to run 100 miles."

Rusty should have known the second the words left his mouth I was not going to let him off the hook on this one. For months he teetered back and forth. He was pretty sure he wanted to do it, but not sure he wanted to do it by himself.

One night in November, we were at Breakthrough Urban Ministries, where Rusty was then running their youth sports ministry. We were with some friends from church serving dinner at their homeless shelter when it happened. I blurted, "I'm in. I'll run it with you."

Two years earlier my close friend and mentor Tim Hoekstra wanted to run fifty miles to celebrate his fiftieth birthday. He had the idea to run 23.8 miles from a Chicago suburb to the start of the Chicago Marathon. Not only did he do it, but he also raised over $50,000 for clean water, and got to run the last 26.2 miles with hundreds of Team World Vision teammates. If we were going to run 100 miles, I wanted to follow in Tim's footsteps and do it at the Chicago Marathon.

Two months later, I was in Phoenix getting ready to run a marathon there. Hannah had gotten married two weeks after we ran Comrades and moved to Phoenix with her husband, Joel, and was going to run the marathon with us. It had been six months since Comrades and since we'd run a race together. We met Hannah and Joel at the expo to pick up our packets, and I told her what Rusty and I were planning to do, this crazy 100-mile thing. How we were going to run 74 miles through the night to the start line of the Chicago Marathon. She had two words for me: "I'm in."

A few weeks later, I sat down to breakfast with JVR to ask for some help. I needed someone to host the Team World Vision team dinner for the Chicago Marathon. For the first time in six years since Team World Vision started, I wouldn't be at the pre-race dinner to help encourage and inspire our team, nearly 1,000 runners, all running to help kids in Africa have clean water. No, this year I would be out on the running path with Rusty and Hannah.

Just as I was about to ask JVR to host the team dinner, he piped up: "I'm in!"

What? What did he mean, he's in? I wasn't even going to ask him to 'be in.' I guess I should have known better than to think JVR was going to sit this one out so he could host a dinner party.

JVR had gotten so used to my crazy ideas he didn't even hesitate. He was in before I finished the thought. I could have asked him to do just about anything with me, and he would have said yes. Especially if it meant we were going to run ridiculously far to help kids in Africa.

JVR grew up in Johannesburg, South Africa. He lived a sheltered life in the suburbs of Joburg, oblivious to the extreme poverty people suffered in townships just a few miles from his home and in the rural countryside. Since coming to the U.S., a tension had been growing in him, a question really. He began asking, "What is my role in global poverty, in meeting the needs of the poor?"

Team World Vision had been just the answer he was looking for. JVR was never a runner. But he has always loved a challenge. JVR and I got close quickly. In 2006, he was one of the first 100 to run the Chicago Marathon as part of Team World Vision's inaugural team. It changed his life.

I met Rusty in 2008 when he started attending the same church as me. He was in the middle of a very tough year. His high school sweetheart had just broken his heart, and he moved to Chicago to work with homeless men at a shelter run by Breakthrough Urban Ministries. He was in the middle of battling his own depression while trying to help these men whose worries seemed much deeper than a broken heart.

Rusty and I had gone to the same college, but he was ten years younger than me. He was a basketball player he told me, NOT a runner. "Running is dumb," he'd say. "It only serves as punishment for real sports."

Six months later, he ran with us in the Chicago Marathon. The next year, we did most of our training together.

I met Hannah in 2006. It was marathon week. We had a special guest from Ethiopia spending the week with us, Gezehgne Abera, the 2000 Olympic marathon gold medalist from Ethiopia. He was here to support the 100 runners we had doing the marathon that weekend. Hannah was on the North Park University cross country team. I brought Abera to talk to her team. She stood out because she seemed more interested than anyone else in what we were trying to do, this Team World Vision thing, running for kids in Africa. A few years later she would skip her senior cross country season to run the marathon with us. She trained with me and Rusty in the "fast" pace group on the lakefront, my therapy group the summer after we lost my brother David. And Hannah ran Comrades with us that next summer, two weeks before graduating college. Three weeks before getting married.

I have two South African friends named Paul who ran Comrades with me — Paul JVR and Paul Courtney. I tried to convince Paul Courtney to run the 100 miles with us, but this time his answer was no. He had run back-to-back Comrades with me, but this time he said he'd serve as our sweeper. He'd plan to run the last 50 miles of the 100 with us and run with whichever of the 4 of us might run into problems. Some tough questions had to be asked. So Paul Courtney asked them.

"What's your plan if someone goes down and can't finish?"

"It won't happen," I told him.

"I know. But what if it does? What's the plan? Will the other three of you keep going? What if someone trips while running in the dark of the night and twists their ankle and simply cannot run?"

"It won't happen," I said.

"It could. You need a plan," Paul insisted. "A way to keep that person involved. Get them ahead on the course to watch the others finish. You need a plan. Of what you will do if someone bonks at mile eighty. Will you separate? Will you wait for them? That's going to be tough, trying to keep four people on the exact same pace for 100 miles. You don't just need a Plan B. You need Plans C thru H too."

Paul Courtney had a point. We needed plans. So we made them. We called a team meeting and talked about contingency plans. How much of the run would we plan to stick together for? At what point would we decide to leave someone. The hardest part: how would we time our arrival at the starting line within our allotted ten-minute window of error? This would require that we predict for four people a pace we could all manage for seventy-four miles, together.

It was a pace we had to keep. If we didn't, we would risk arriving too early and having to sit around at the starting line while our muscles locked up. If we arrived late, we risked not being allowed to start the race. If we cut the seventy-four short before the start of the race, we would have to finish the Chicago Marathon and then make up the miles we had missed.

Our basic plan:

1. Do everything we can to run the first 74 miles together.
2. Arrive at the starting line to join 45,000 other runners, including nearly 1,000 Team World Vision teammates.

3. Be among the last people to cross the starting line, to avoid a lot of standing around.
4. To do this, we need to arrive between 8:05 and 8:15 AM. The race started at 7:30 AM, but it usually takes 45 minutes to get everyone across the starting line.

Four people. Seventy-four miles.

A ten-minute window of error. To get to the starting line, together.

It sounded doable.

If we could get to the start line, with seventy-four miles behind us, we could separate if we needed to. We'd have the crowds along the course, 45,000 other runners, and our other Team World Vision teammates to help us get through. We couldn't wait to feel the energy at the start line. It would be the best feeling in the world.

For Rusty, training was tiring. Not the distance, but the early mornings. He didn't want all of these long runs to impact his work at Breakthrough Urban Ministries or his wife, Anna. So he started a lot of his runs at 4 a.m., some even earlier.

For Hannah, training was lonely. When we trained for Comrades, she lived in Chicago and had the rest of the team to train with. Now, here she was, living in Phoenix, doing 30-mile runs alone in 102-degree heat.

For JVR training was good. It wasn't great. It wasn't like the year before when we were all training for Comrades, when he always had someone to do his long runs with. But training was good.

For me, training was an experiment. I was the only one on the 100-mile team that was going back to run Comrades. This meant training to run the 56-mile ultramarathon at the end of May, recovering, then ramping back up to 100-mile training. I considered wearing a shirt at Comrades that said, "Comrades is a training run," but Paul Courtney told me it wasn't such a good idea. Pretty sure he was right.

After Comrades that May, I didn't run a step for five weeks. Just what Bart Yasso had told me to do. When it comes to training, Bart is the authority. After the first week of July, one day short of five weeks, I started training again. I only had to do a few long runs according to Bart. My first couple of weeks back, I jumped right into distance.

My biggest week of training:

» 40 miles on Sunday night with JVR and Rusty.
» 8 miles on Tuesday by myself.
» 26.2 miles on Thursday with Rusty. Starting at 3 a.m.
» 26.2 miles on Friday with Rusty.

My first ever 100-mile week. I felt good. It was tough. But I felt good.

Uh-oh. A 100-mile week? And I felt good about that? I was planning to run 100 miles in one day. It was at that point I started getting a little nervous.

Race Day: Saturday, 4:30 p.m., Chicago Marathon Expo

The Chicago Marathon didn't start until fifteen hours after we would begin running. The energy was electric as we stood at our own little starting line on the Chicago lakefront path, surrounded by friends and family ready to send us off.

The first couple of hours seemed to fly by. Ten miles in we stopped by the Team World Vision dinner to encourage our teammates. As we left the team dinner, Hannah's husband, Joel, my brother, Dan, and Rusty's dad, Russ, joined us on bikes. They would be our support crew through the late hours in the night.

Shortly after sunset, JVR's friends began showing up on the lakefront to run a few miles with us.

It was awesome. We couldn't believe how well things were going. That is until mile forty.

JVR had a bit of meltdown. He sat down on the side of path. He felt like he couldn't take one more step. He looked like he couldn't take one more step. He was so tired. He wasn't sure if he could go on.

Eric Schoonveld, a member of our bike crew, handed JVR a thermos of chicken soup. It was perfect. He said it tasted like heaven. He was back. For now.

Then around 2 o'clock, in the middle of the night, Rusty and I had a little tiff about doing math problems. Rusty wanted to do math problems to keep our minds occupied. He kept calling it "Midnight Math." I was not feeling well. And I definitely was not feeling Rusty's midnight math idea.

"Rusty! I'm not going to do midnight math! Stop saying it! Stop! I don't want to do math problems right now!"

I know Rusty was a little shocked. He and I always do math problems on long runs to kill time. But I was hitting a rough patch around mile 50, so Rusty thought he'd lighten the mood. Apparently, he found out, I don't love doing math problems as much as he thought I did. Well, not at 2:30 in the morning on mile 50 of 100.

The night was beautiful. Few people ever get to experience the Chicago lakefront path at 3:30 in the morning. The skyline reflected in Lake Michigan, the breeze off the lake to cool us off from the unseasonably warm October weather.

My brother Dan and Rusty's dad (Papa Russ) stayed with us through the entire night. Sometimes we talked. Sometimes we ran in silence for what seemed like an eternity. Just putting one foot in front of the other.

Friends met us during the wee hours to encourage us, to run with us, to witness our insanity.

Just when it seemed the night would never end, the sun made a slow appearance over Lake Michigan. I couldn't believe we were pulling it off. It had been a long night. There were a few times I was nervous we wouldn't get there.

There were moments that night when one or the other of us looked like we wouldn't make it to the starting line. But as we ran into Grant Park to meet up with the big team for the Team World Vision pep rally, I realized we were right on schedule. We ran a giant circle around the hundreds of Team World Vision runners who were getting ready for the team picture, slapping their hands. We jumped in for the team picture, did the Team World Vision rally clap and were off. We still had six miles to run before the start of the race. But we were right on schedule. So far, so good.

Leaving the pep rally we could tell JVR was starting to struggle again. I had lost track of who was eating what and when. But it was starting to show. Maybe it was the pace we had kept. The painkillers he took. Maybe he wasn't drinking enough. He was hurting. At least we were getting to the start line on time, together. Once we got there, the crowds would carry us. Our plan would work. We could all do our own thing if we had to, and we'd have plenty of people around us to keep us going. We were doing it.

The Marathon to Beat All Marathons

"If something can go wrong, it probably will."

MURPHY'S LAW

What happened next brought our world to a standstill. My stomach dropped so hard, I felt it to my core. Like someone had punched me in the gut. How was this possible? We had done everything right. We were right on schedule. We had run all night for this moment. The moment where we would join 45,000 runners at the start line of the Chicago Marathon and their energy would carry us the last 26.2 miles. This couldn't be happening. Not now. Not after all it took to get here.

I felt overwhelmed with despair. Where was everyone?

Apparently our plan had one small glitch. The marathon had done the best job ever getting everyone across the starting line. In past years, it took forty-five minutes from the time the starting gun sounded for the last people in the sea of runners to get up to the starting line. This year they had done it in twenty-eight. When we arrived, there was no one there. Every runner had been gone at least ten minutes. Everything was shutting down. The starting line was a ghost town.

I could see it on Paul Courtney's face, the doubt. The thought of, "uh-oh, guys, this doesn't look so good." But he needed to stay calm, for the team. He had twenty-four miles in to our seventy-four. It would be up to him to think clearly. To encourage us. To keep us from giving in to the voices. The voices that whisper to you in times like this, "Just quit. It's too hard. You can't do it. Just. Give. Up."

He knew the voices would start soon. He had heard them himself plenty of times. He knew we were counting on the crowd of runners to pull us the last twenty-six miles. We weren't going to get that kind of help this day. So Paul Courtney would have to stay calm and be that kind of friend. The kind who looks you in the face and tells you not to worry, that it will work out, that you can do it. The kind of friend that lies to you.

Dave Louthan, the Charity Director for the marathon, spotted us, and led us through the starting-line area making sure we were allowed to start the race. But it was eerie to say the least.

The first mile seemed like something from an apocalypse movie, one where all of mankind had disappeared except a few people. And we were the only people left on the planet. We even had big monstrous machines to battle, as giant street-sweepers flooded the street cleaning up the mess that is left when 45,000 people go down a Chicago city street inside of twenty-eight minutes.

JVR wasn't looking good. This had hit him hard. He was walking.

"Don't worry, guys," Paul Courtney told us, trying to sound positive. "You'll catch the chase vehicle. You will. I'm guessing around mile eight or ten."

"WHAT?" I thought, "Mile eight or ten? We have to run alone. No fans. No aid stations. No one else. For eight to ten more miles? I wasn't sure we even knew the route. What if we didn't?"

We kept trying to stay together, but it just wasn't happening. JVR kept yelling for us to go on without him. He'd finish. He promised.

At mile seventy-seven, the five of us huddled together. We had some decisions to make. Some tough decisions.

I was sick to my stomach. Literally. I couldn't do it. I couldn't leave JVR. Not like this. I started crying. Then I looked up and saw Jan, a former Team World Vision coach and friend of JVR.

She was wearing street clothes. She wasn't running. She was there waiting to cheer us on.

"Jan! Can you run?"

She didn't hesitate. She climbed the barricade that separated the spectators from the runners and said she would run with Paul Courtney and JVR.

As we left JVR, tears stained my cheeks. Even though we knew it was not likely we would all finish the entire 100 miles at the same time, it felt like we were abandoning our brother.

Rusty, Hannah, and I caught the chase vehicle at mile three. Right at the first Team World Vision cheer station. It was there I saw Timmy. When he saw me he asked, "What can I do for you man?"

"I need you to run with me."

He could tell I was serious. So he ran with us.

Mile 82, AKA Chicago Marathon Mile 8

JVR needed food and Paul Courtney knew where to get it. He left for just a few minutes to find a gas station to buy something for JVR to eat. It shouldn't be hard to catch back up to him, or so he thought. But when he got back to the race course just a few minutes later, JVR was nowhere in sight. Paul Courtney ran up the course a half mile. No JVR. He ran back a ways. No JVR.

He finally found him in the Mile 8 medical tent.

"Sir! How far have you run?" the EMT asked. JVR responded, "Eighty-two miles."

The Marathon to Beat All Marathons   231

"Oh no. This guy's delirious," the EMT said to a co-worker. "Sir! How far have you run TODAY?"

JVR gave the same response: "Eighty-two miles."

The EMT called for backup. "Jim, this guy is bad. Worst I've seen today. He's hallucinating. He keeps saying he has run eight-two miles."

Luckily for JVR, the other medic had watched us on the news the day before. He ran over to help.

"I think he's telling the truth," the guy said. "Are you one of the Team World Vision 100-milers?"

For a guy who had only run eight miles, JVR looked like crap. But for a guy who had run eighty-two, he just looked like a guy who had run eighty-two. They gave him some salt tablets and sent him on his way.

Around the marathon halfway point, mile eighty-seven for our group, Rusty, Hannah, and I all ran into the porta-potties. When we came out, we huddled together again on the side of the road. We needed a pep talk. I guess it was my turn. I looked Rusty and Hannah in the eyes. Hannah's were filling with tears. Rusty's were hidden by his sunglasses. I knew they were both feeling the same way I was feeling. Beat.

"We got this. We have got this. We will make it. We. Will. Do. This!"

You learn a lot about someone running 100 miles with them.

Rusty gets quiet when he hits a rough patch.

JVR gets determined.

Hannah doesn't seem to hit them very often.

I get irritable.

At mile ninety-five, I had my second temper tantrum. The first had been when Rusty wouldn't stop talking about doing math problems at two a.m.

I was hitting the wall. Not bad I thought. Mile 95 and I was just hitting the wall? But man, that was some wall.

"I need to walk," I told them.

Rusty and Hannah tried to get me pumped up. Telling me I could do it. Telling me we should start running. Telling me all sorts of things I just couldn't listen to. Not at that moment.

"Stop! Stop! Stop talking!" I literally put my hands over my ears as I yelled at them like a five-year-old having a temper tantrum.

Then, out of nowhere. I took off running. Fast.

They must have thought I was nuts. One minute I'm yelling because I want to keep walking. Then I take off sprinting, weaving through the other marathoners. So, Hannah and Rusty took off after me. They knew there was no way I could keep this pace very long.

My surge lasted about a half-mile. Then, more walking. At least that's what I call it. I'm a good three or four inches taller than Rusty, and nearly a foot taller than Hannah. Rusty calls me Sergio because I run in surges and can't hold a steady pace. And he calls me Turbo when I walk, because I walk so fast that he physically can't keep up if he walks. So he'd run past me. Then walk until I caught him again. "It's not a rest if you walk so fast," Rusty always tells me.

At mile 96, something moved in me. Not emotionally, it was something else. I had to go. Bad. Ninety-six miles into a 100-mile run, just four miles to go. You would think I'd just wait. But that wasn't going to happen. I told my brother, Dan, to run ahead and find me a place to use the bathroom. When I walked into the antique shop in Chinatown, the owner changed her mind quickly about letting me use the bathroom. I must have been some sight.

 The Marathon to Beat All Marathons   233

Covered in sweat. No shirt. Salt all over my face. And panic too.

"No, no, no, no, no, no, no, no!" she cried in a thick Mandarin accent. Oh, yeah. She had definitely changed her mind.

"Ma'am. Either he can use your bathroom. Or he might go right here on your floor," my brother told her.

She conceded. I'm sure she came to regret it.

By this time, Hannah was well ahead of us and not sure how far we had fallen back. One minute we were right behind her, the next she couldn't see us anymore.

She decided to run to the second to last turn, at the bottom of the hill on Roosevelt and then wait for us.

Five or ten minutes later, maybe a little more, we saw her. She was just standing there in the middle of the road, facing the wrong way, runners going past her, fans yelling for her to keep running, legs tightening up, while she just stood there looking for us. After running 99.5 miles she stopped to wait for us. When we reached her, we wanted to run, but after standing there, Hannah's legs had locked up. "Sorry boys. I waited for you here, now you gotta walk this hill with me." Hannah scolded us with a smile, tears welling up in her eyes.

21 hours, 35 minutes

Hannah, Rusty, and I crossed the finish line together. It was painful. It was awesome. I don't remember much about the long, slow, painful, one-mile walk back to the Team World Vision tent. Hugs. Tears. And the thought of a sign Rusty's wife had held out for us on the course. A sign that read, "One day, you will not be able to run 100 miles. Today is not that day."

On the long walk back down Lake Shore Drive to the Team World Vision tent, I lost Rusty and Hannah. I was alone. I knew the tent would be filled with hundreds of our teammates who had just finished the marathon. Dani would be there. My brother would be there. I couldn't process everything and began tearing up. I stepped off the sidewalk, put my hands on my knees and started sobbing. For maybe four or five minutes, I allowed myself to just be there, by myself, to take a moment to be alone. To be *runmotional*.

Then, I continued the long slow painful walk. At the tent, reunited with Rusty and Hannah, we anxiously awaited news about JVR. We were more than a little concerned. JVR told us he would not quit. But he had been in pretty bad shape when we left him.

Paul Courtney told me later that JVR had looked bad. But the medics checked him a few times and kept releasing him back out on the course. They were making their way to the finish line, and actually making better time than they thought.

We hadn't been back at the Team World Vision tent long when the call came from Paul Courtney. He and JVR were a quarter-mile from the finish line. I yelled to Hannah and Rusty, "Let's go! We gotta watch JVR finish!"

Rusty couldn't cover the fifty yards we had to walk to where we could watch JVR finish. He was just too spent.

I tell JVR I was there at the finish line when he came across. But he says, "It's all a blur. I was hurting. I told you guys I would finish. I had no idea what it would take. I had no idea I would have to dig so deep."

"I've never seen anything like it," Paul Courtney told me. "The guy has more guts than anyone I've ever met."

An hour later, we were still lying on the ground outside the Team World Vision tent, beaten, broken. That's when I remember hearing Mac tell us JVR needed to go to the hospital.

After the race I laid there for hours, in Grant Park just a stone's throw from the Team World Vision tent. The ground was cold beneath me and the tinfoil space blanket did little to keep me warm. Every few minutes, the sun would peek through the clouds and warm my face for a moment, then disappear again behind the clouds. I felt a deep sense of peace. I felt cold. I felt spent. I felt like someone had smashed my feet with a sledgehammer.

Rusty disappeared. One minute he was lying there on the ground ten feet from me. Then he was gone. Turns out he had gone home and then threw up in the shower.

I couldn't even walk 100 yards to where Dani pulled our car up to the curb, so she had to drive it right into Grant Park so I could climb in.

Hannah couldn't stand. She had to be carried to a car, then carried to her room. She spent a night in the hospital with what appeared to be a torn calf muscle. It wasn't.

JVR had to be taken to the hospital and put into the intensive care unit. His kidneys had completely shut down. His blood was a thick sludge. Within twenty-four hours, he had put on 25 pounds as they pumped him full of fluids that his body failed to process.

Had we pushed him too hard? Had he pushed himself too far?

With JVR in the hospital, I was getting very little sleep. I have had enough of hospitals in my life and hated seeing one of my best friends laying there, his body destroyed from what we had put ourselves through, what we had put him through.

After nearly a week in the ICU, they tried moving him to a regular room. During the transition, he had several severe seizures and was immediately put back in ICU. Just when I thought I could take no more, things took a turn for the better. His kidneys started working again. Exactly two weeks after we ran 100 miles, JVR was released from the hospital. I was on a plane for Kenya to see the kids we had run for, to see Maurine and her family. I didn't get to see him out of the hospital until two weeks later when I returned.

JVR made a full recovery. A year later he actually ran the Chicago marathon with Team World Vision.

Ask any one of us if we had to do it all over again, would we? In a heartbeat we'd all say yes. Ask us if we will ever run 100 miles again. That's a completely different question.

Relentless Forward Motion

"The race does not always go to the swift, but to the ones who keep running."

ANONYMOUS

Someone once told me it's about relentless forward motion. They were talking about running ultramarathons. But as it is with most things running, it was about much more than that.

When we lost my dad, it felt like I was standing still for so long. Within days most of the people who had been at the funeral had gone back to life as usual. Within weeks, even the closest of friends seemed to be doing okay. People were moving. The world was moving. But I was standing still.

You can't finish a race standing still. You have to keep moving. Sometimes you move fast. Sometimes you move slowly. The tougher the race, the more important it is to keep moving forward, relentlessly.

The pain in this life can be unbearable. The fear of the unknown is paralyzing. You think, "I can't go on. Not like this. Things will never be the same, and I don't know if I can keep doing this. Not now. Maybe not ever."

When faced with loss, whether the loss of a dream, a broken relationship, divorce, death of a loved one or even something more terrible than these, it does little to have people offer cliché consolations. "It's all part of God's plan," they say. They mean well, but they are often just rubbing salt in the wound.

In *A Grief Observed*, C.S. Lewis wrote:

> *"Talk to me about the truth of religion and I'll listen gladly. Talk to me about the duty of religion and I'll listen submissively. But don't come talking to me about the consolations of religion or I shall suspect that you don't understand."*

While the world is moving forward and you are standing still you will, at some point, need to make a decision. That is, as much as a hopeless person can hope to make decisions. Will you stay there, standing still, or will you, somehow, begin moving again, living again?

Lewis concluded by writing:

> *"Reality never repeats. The exact same thing is never taken away and given back.... For that is what we should all like. The happy past restored."*

It is true life will never be the same again. The happy past will never be restored. Life will never be as good as it might have been if Dad and David were still here. But life can still be good. Still, joy can be alive in my life. Pain will come. Sometimes it will stay. It's not so much that I have to change, but rather change my perspective, my expectations. I have tried to stop asking God why all this pain exists in this world, and instead try to get busy doing something about it. I am mindful now to keep moving with relentless forward motion.

Consultation Room

"I don't know what tomorrow might bring, but I'm still hoping no matter what it is, it's gonna be better than today."

BLAZE OLAMIDAY

"Chitwood family, the doctor would like to see you in the consultation room please," said the nurse at the Ft. Wayne Hospital to my mom, my sister-in-law, Kim, and me. There is no way that meeting the doctor in the consultation room could mean anything good. I braced myself for the worst news.

We had been at the hospital all day while my brother Dan was having a quintuple bypass. The fifty-foot walk to the consultation room felt like a mile. As the three of us sat waiting for the doctor, I rehearsed in my mind what I would say to Kim and my mom when the doctor inevitably came in and told us that Dan had not made it through the surgery.

How could I possibly handle this myself, let alone watch Kim and my mom get this kind of news? I couldn't think of any possible reason they would call us into the consultation room for anything other than bad news.

This quintuple bypass surgery just didn't make sense. Sure Dan could stand to lose a few pounds, maybe eat a little less fast food. But he's an Ironman for crying out loud. Quintuple bypass? Seriously?

Before he went into surgery, the doctors described how they were going to crack open his rib cage and stop his heart. They would keep his blood pumping and lungs breathing with a machine, and fix his arteries with blood vessels from his leg. Then, they'd jump start his heart and close him up with some heavy-duty wires. I almost passed out listening to them describe the surgery.

If I wasn't nervous before, I was nervous now.

Timmy knew I was worried about the surgery. He knew hospitals are not exactly my favorite place to be. So, he came with me to Ft. Wayne. Our little posse of family and friends held vigil in the waiting room for hours. We ate hospital food and waited anxiously for news. And now this, getting called into the consultation room. This couldn't be good.

After waiting for what felt like an eternity, the doctor walked in. I could tell almost immediately the news was not what I had feared. Everything was okay. Dan had done well and was in the recovery room.

Borrowed Time

"Time is at once the most valuable and the most perishable of all our possessions."

JOHN RANDOLPH

I was on a conference call for work with a couple of guys I didn't know well. I can't tell you what their names were, but Rusty was there with me, talking to these guys about running Comrades with us; about going to Kenya to see some water projects. My caller ID popped up with my sister-in-law's name, Kim Chitwood. I figured it was my brother Dan calling from her phone because his battery died, or he left it at home, or some other reason that seemed to make sense as to why Kim's name was popping up on my phone. I hit ignore. "I'll call him back right after this meeting," I thought.

Immediately the name appeared on the phone again. Dan usually calls twice in a row. He figured I must have taken too long to find my phone, which was often the case. He usually doesn't leave a message until the second call. I hit ignore, again. And then, her name popped up a third time, immediately.

"Guys, I'm sorry, I need to take this call."

At first all I could hear was crying on the other end of the line. It's Kim, not Dan. She's sobbing and trying to tell me something, but it's hard to understand what she's saying. She's barely able to get the words out. Finally she says words that make sense, even though they don't make any sense at all.

"Michael, Dan flat-lined." She cries through panic and tears.

"I don't know what happened. He just flat-lined." She says. "I'm sorry, the paramedics are here. I have to go. I'll call you back."

This room I'm in. Why is it spinning so fast? My head is on the table and I can't breathe. I'm screaming and I can't breathe. Wait, is that me on the floor? It is, I can see myself, on my knees on the floor of the conference room at my office, my fist going through the wall.

I see Rusty out of the corner of my eye, he's standing over me. Suddenly my friends are all around me, I can tell they are there, but I'm not sure who they are. Their faces are blurred together. At least a few of them are crying too, asking me what's going on, but I can't answer, I can't form any words, I'm just crying and hyperventilating. I just need to breathe.

They form a circle around me, and some of their hands are on me. I'm sitting in a chair now, my office chair, and someone's praying. All I can think is, "I've got to get out of this dream. I've got to get out of this dream. This has got to be a bad dream."

I can hope and pray all I want, but this is not a dream. When they are finished praying, the tears stop momentarily, I slowly lift my head, and all I can say is, "I need to go home and pack."

Rusty drives me in my own car to my house and on the way there my phone rings again and I see only a first name on the caller ID, Bruce. Bruce is my brother Dan's best friend and on staff at the church that Dan pastors. I waste no time answering his call.

"Bruce, is he gone?"

"Yeah, buddy. He's gone. I'm so sorry."

An all-too-familiar fog settled over me as I packed my bag and prepared for the three-and-a-half-hour drive from Chicago to Ft. Wayne. I knew the fog would not lift anytime soon. My heart sank as I readied myself for the long road ahead. Not the drive to Indiana, but the long road of grief and pain that has become one I know too well; the getting stuck, and trying to get unstuck; the sadness that settles over everything; the late-night dreams and waking up sobbing uncontrollably. The pain of loss is like no other pain. I tell God that I'm just not ready for this again, not yet.

Dan died eighteen months after his heart surgery. The docs said he was doing great. It didn't make any sense. He had just grilled up some burgers for the kids and went upstairs to get ready for his daughter Danni's eighth-grade basketball game. He never came back downstairs.

When a loved one is torn from us, we are left with the unanswerable question that seems to sink its claws deep into our every thought and amplifies the pain; just one simple word. "Why?"

To which there is no answer. At least none that would suffice.

In the eighteen months following his surgery, Dan lived a lot of life. He celebrated the tenth anniversary of the church he pastored and moved the church into its own building for the first time. He saw his oldest daughter, Taylor, graduate high school, go to college, and be healed of the seizures she had battled for six years. He got to watch his son Jordan's senior football season and help him get his driver's license. He watched his son Payton play football and join the wrestling team, and saw his daughter Danni run cross country and play basketball. He got to compete in another half Ironman triathlon. He baptized people, dedicated babies, officiated weddings, and even some funerals. And he got to spend eighty-five more Fridays with the love of his life, his wife Kim. Dan lived a lot in those eighteen months.

I'd be lying if I said I'm not angry. I am. Or if I pretended that it makes sense in any way at all. It doesn't. But I do know I am grateful for the extra time we got with Dan. When I sat in that consultation room after his heart surgery just eighteen months ear-lier, I was certain we had lost him. But we hadn't lost him yet. We got a chance that many people aren't afforded. We got just a little more time.

At All Costs

"The aim of the wise is not to secure pleasure, but to avoid pain."

ARISTOTLE

We are all hard-wired to avoid pain at all costs. It is a basic survival instinct for all animals. We humans, however, have the instinct to not just avoid physical pain, but to avoid pain in all its forms, many of which, because of how we were divinely created, we have a unique capacity to feel.

We learn, over time, the things that hurt us, that cause us pain, and we create a set of boundaries that grow out of lessons learned the hard way, the painful way. Burn yourself on the stove enough times and eventually you learn not to touch a hot stove. This works when the cause of pain is predictable. But what happens when you have no control over when the stove is on or off? What happens if there are no indicators to help you decide whether it's safe to touch? What if the stove burned you in a seemingly random fashion? You might just decide it's not worth it to ever go near the stove again. Not worth the unpredictable risk of pain.

The ability to see the potential for pain in given situations, to see a few steps down the road and adjust course accordingly, is a safeguard for us. It helps us avoid pain, if and when it can be avoided.

People who have spent limited time with me might think I am Captain Positive, always encouraging, always risking, always taking on challenges regardless of fear. They think, "This guy used to be a big, overweight football player who hated running, and he just ran 100 miles in a day. This guy quit his job and took a risk to help start up a charity running team. This guy doesn't let a little thing like fear get in his way."

They have an idea of who I am, so when they really get to know me, to see beyond the surface, that image is shattered. They get caught off-guard when I share my fears with them. My hurt. My pain.

God knew we'd be racked with fear too. There are dozens of references throughout Scripture imploring us not to fear. It's not that I never let fear keep me from taking risks. It's because of the pain I have experienced that I know which things are truly worth being afraid of.

One day Rusty and I were out on a run and the issue of having kids came up. Dani and I had been married for eleven years and still had not decided whether or not we wanted to have kids. Rusty started asking questions and got answers he wasn't expecting and hadn't bargained for.

"Sure, we've thought a lot about having kids," I told him, "but we just aren't sure it's worth all the pain."

Pain? Who leads into a conversation about having kids talking about the pain of it?

Even though Rusty and I had been friends for five years, he had never really heard the story of how I lost my dad until a few weeks earlier. Over dinner one night, I told him about the pain of losing my dad, and watched his heart break for me. I felt our friendship grow deeper when I saw the empathy he felt for my loss. He shared he has never lost someone close to him, never felt the aching emptiness left in the absence of a loved one. Rusty was living in the *before*.

I was living in the *after*.

For me, having kids represented an intentional decision to enter head-on into an adventure guaranteed to bring undisclosed amounts of heartache and pain. I couldn't imagine why someone would sign up for that.

Many people would try to tell me the joy of having a child far outweighs the pain, and I would think them foolish, or ignorant, assuming they had obviously not yet felt the stomach-wrenching hurt that is bound to come to us all eventually.

I would think to myself:

> *Sure, you can say it's worth it. You've never watched a homeless ten-year-old fall asleep in class reeking of poverty, hopelessness in her eyes. You've never seen a child walk for water that will make her sick and seen the tears in her mother's eyes because she has already lost two children to that dirty water and doesn't think she can survive the loss of another. Of course you think it's worth it. You haven't watched a man lay in the mud, discarded by his community, left to beg, left to rot, left to die.*

> *You've never watched your father die and your mother feel so lost without him that you worry relentlessly if she will ever recover a sense of normalcy in her life, ever feel joy again. You've never watched your brother battle alcoholism and morbid obesity, watched him lose that battle and leave a wife, four kids, his mother, and two brokenhearted brothers behind. And faced that loss again. And then just one brokenhearted brother.*
> *Of course you think it's worth the risk. You've never*

been pregnant and so excited to be a parent that you can't help envisioning birthdays and family vacations to Disney World, and soccer games, and concerts, and first dates, and proms, and graduations, a wedding, and all the joy that comes with being a mother and a father, only to be told you lost the baby.

Sure you think it's worth it, because you have yet to feel the real pain that awaits us all. You have yet to be burned.

The sum of these imaginary arguments in my own soul came out in a cluttered mess that sounded a lot like excuses. Excuses and fear. And though Rusty had not been the one to make these arguments, he was the one who caught the brunt of my hurt and frustration. This is the earful Rusty got the day he asked me if Dani and I wanted to have kids. For a moment, I thought I had lost his respect entirely. He'd been bamboozled. I was not who he thought I was at all. Surely he was disappointed.

"I've never heard you talk so negative before, bro. This just doesn't sound like you," he told me.

The argument I was making was incredibly self-centered. It presumed either my pain was unique and therefore I was justified in my attempts to avoid any further injury at all costs, or that if in fact others had experienced the type of loss, or pain, or hopelessness I have experienced, they would either come to the same conclusions about further exposure, or they must be fools.

Like I said, a lot of times people expect me to be Captain Positive, and the truth is, a lot of the time, I am. Despite the hurt and pain this life has for us, I still believe life can be incredible. I still believe in a loving God who thinks I'm special. I still believe that, even though no special moment in my life will be as special as it would have been if my dad and my brothers could have shared it with me, there can still be special moments.

Thankfully Rusty didn't give up on me. "Michael, God wants you to have the trust in Him that you had when you lived in the *before*, even when you are living in the *after*."

After that conversation with Rusty, I took a deep look inside myself, and I had some tough conversations with God. I realized I needed to take a bit of my own advice. So I asked myself the question I first asked Steve Spear when I invited him to run Comrades, and have since asked many others: "Other than fear, what is holding you back?"

Honestly. It was only fear that was holding me back. A justified fear maybe, but fear nonetheless.

When it came to just about anything in life, I was willing to take risks, to step through fear to get to the good stuff.

"Almost every good thing God has for us in this life lays just on the other side of fear."

I had said this so many times.

It's true, we are not in control. We cannot always prevent pain. We may get pretty good at predicting where it might strike, but despite our best efforts to avoid those situations, it will come. We cannot avoid it. Cannot. So I will decide not to try avoiding it.

Instead, I will risk when I feel called to risk. I will dare when the Spirit invites me to dare. I will step through fear, despite the screaming voice in my ear telling me only hurt and pain await me, and instead I will listen to the quiet whisper telling me, "I love you. You can do this. It's worth the risk."

Instead of predicting the worst that can happen, I will believe in the best possibilities, not blind to the risks, but in spite of them.

I will heed my own advice and step through the fear, because I believe everything great, everything incredible, everything worth experiencing, every amazing thing God has for us in this life lays just on the other side of fear.

One More Conversation

"We shall draw from the heart of suffering itself the means of inspiration and survival."

WINSTON CHURCHILL

The week before Dan died, he texted me:

"Hey man, would you have time to FaceTime with me today? Even just a few minutes. Nothing bad. Just spending time with God this morning, and He's reminding me about the need to re-charge my battery and refresh my spirit. I have a list of identified things that do this. One of them is 'Spending time with Michael either in person or on the phone.' Love ya, man."

Later that day we spent an hour and a half video chatting. It was an amazing gift.

It had taken Dani and I thirteen years to decide to have kids. The pain we had faced through the loss of our dads and my brother David had kept us paralyzed, afraid to step into the unknown. We got pregnant two months after we took the leap of faith, and we were devastated when Dani had a miscarriage.

Dani and I had always wanted to adopt and decided to get started with the process. It had been a cool thing to share with Dan because he and Kim had adopted my niece Danni. (Try to keep 'em straight now — Dan my brother, Danni my niece, and Dani my wife.) Just when we were almost through the home study, Dani (my wife) got pregnant again.

That day, in one of my last conversations with Dan, we talked mostly about parenthood. We laughed a lot and, as usual, he was a huge source of encouragement. I decided to tell him the names we had picked out for a boy or a girl. Two days later he called me, and the first thing he said was, "Michael. I'll be super pumped whether you have a boy or a girl. But I'm rooting for a boy. I just love the name you picked out. Cruz Justice. I'm gonna call him Cruiser."

That was the last conversation we ever had.

Legacy

> *"When I die, let it be with worn-out shoes and empty pockets."*
>
> RUSTY FUNK

The sky is the clearest blue I have ever seen and the clouds seem to be at a stand still. Maurine's bare feet touch each rock for less than a moment as she races with me down the path near her home, reaching for my hand and lifting my heart with her smile. She has grown up so much in the last few years. She is now seven, and she knows me like family. The water she drinks is clean, the malaria is gone, her school is one of the best in the region. Her mother, Josphine, greets me with a big smile and hug each day I am here, and her brother, Justine, is graduating from college this year, the first in his family.

Everything has changed.

It's been thirteen years since I lost my dad, five years since we lost David, and just a few months since Dan died. Mile markers of the grief that has left a hole in my heart that will never be fully repaired. A pain that often seems unbearable. But this little girl, Maurine, has revealed to me a joy I had ceased believing could exist in this world, a world that holds so much heartache. I am finding that love is doing the hard work of repairing my broken heart. God is revealing His love for me in the midst of loss and heartbreak, and in the strangest of places. I meet God in the lives of the poor, the broken, in the places one might never think to look.

Tomorrow I leave Kenya and head for home. Every time I say goodbye to this place a part of my heart stays behind, but I am anxious to get home to Dani. Our son is due to be born in less than two months and there's so much to do to prepare for his arrival. Even now I dream about bringing him here to meet his Kenyan family, to spend time in this place and with these people who have forever changed my life.

The trajectory of my life was altered forever when we lost my dad. While that loss was only the beginning of my pain, it was also the impetus for a movement that will honor his legacy. Two years before my dad died, my brother Dan gave him a journal called "A Father's Legacy." He had only written on a handful of pages, but one entry in particular has helped shape my life more than anything I have ever read.

From my dad's journal: October 2000

> *What is the spiritual legacy you would like to leave for others? Why is this important to you?*
> Written on a plane from N.Y. to Detroit 5:50 p.m.

> Several pages in this book were written on my Sierre Leone trip – Oct. 2000. This is my last one on the way home. As I sit here in a first-class seat and think back of the people on the streets of Freetown — the poverty that I have seen in Haiti, Nicaragua, and now in Freetown has forever changed my life. The absolute luxury we enjoy in America is hard to enjoy once you've seen our fellow man living in poverty–not knowing if they will have a next meal–or when they'll have a meal. What spiritual "legacy" do

I want to leave—only that we will remember the poor—and do what we can to relieve their suffering. Oct. 29, 2000

My dad wrote this almost seven months before that call. That call that changed everything. Seven months before my heart was broken. Seven months before my dreams were lost, and my faith was shattered.

My friend Brad once asked me, "If your dad hadn't died, would you be doing what you are doing? Working for World Vision? Helping kids around the world?"

Leave it to a close friend to ask a tough question. Just as we cannot have the precious past restored, we can never know how things might have been. We can only live in the world that is, the circumstances that we have. The truth is that I'm not sure if I would be doing what I'm doing if I had not lost my dad. I can only know that I wish he was here to be a part of it with me. Every race I run is less than it would have been if he were there to watch, through the viewfinder of his camera like he watched every one of my football games.

I may not know whether I would have helped start Team World Vision if we had not lost him, but I do know this — I would not be who I am if I had not had him as my father in the first place. I only pray that I can live up to his challenge: to remember the poor and do what I can to relieve their suffering. As a reminder, I had his words tattooed down my back: *"Remember the poor & Relieve their suffering."*

Running has changed my life in ways that I could never have imagined. God has met me out on the road time and time again. And through Team World Vision, I have had the absolute privilege to take the very thing that has brought me so much healing and use it to help others, to bring clean water to communities like Maurine's. I am grateful that despite the pain and loss and heartache this world has to offer, God can show up in the midst of it and bring healing, and restoration, and redemption. I am grateful today for all God has seen me through and all that is yet to come. And I am grateful to be back here, in my favorite place on earth, underneath the African sky.

Afterward
the BABY COMES

The phone rang. It was Rusty's name on the caller ID. I wasn't sure I could hold it together, but I was desperate to talk to someone. Rusty was in South Africa on his way to the start line of the Comrades ultramarathon, the first one I had missed in five years. He was running on behalf of Team World Vision, doing his part to relieve the suffering of others.

He was calling to check on Dani, to see if our baby had arrived yet. I picked up the phone and that's the moment I realized just exactly how afraid I was that Dani wasn't going to make it, that the baby wasn't going to make it. I'd been here before, and I knew that there are simply no guarantees. I've lost too much to assume everything will always be all right.

Within seconds of hearing Rusty's voice, mine started to shake and the tears started to slowly stream down my face. I told him how Dani was unconscious and hooked up to all sorts of monitors. She had an oxygen mask over her mouth and nose, and she lay motionless as the room filled with a slow, steady beeping noise that brought back fears from thirteen years earlier when those were the final sounds I heard in my dad's hospital room. I was terrified I was going to lose her.

We'd been in the hospital for six days already. Dani had shown signs of preeclampsia, a condition that was putting her life and the baby's at risk. They had been monitoring her weekly because they considered ours a "high-risk pregnancy" since we'd already had one miscarriage and Dani was over 35 years old. Dani's blood pressure kept rising to unsafe levels and the baby's heart rate was showing decelerations, slowing down suddenly. The doctors told us if her blood pressure rose too high, or if the baby's heart rate continued to slow down, they would need to do an emergency C-section.

They had already given Dani heavy pain medication and an epidural, which is why she was drifting in and out of consciousness. I fought back the fears as best I could, but they continued creeping up on me. As I talked to Rusty on the phone from Dani's hospital room, I tried my best to sound like I had it together, but I was trembling with fear, and I'm sure he could tell. He encouraged the best he could from 9,000 miles away in South Africa.

When they finally made the decision to do the C-section, things began moving quickly. Dani had already been in labor for 36 hours. Her blood pressure had reached the red zone, and the baby's heart rate had continued to slow. It was time.

I sat on a stool so I could look Dani in the eye as she lay motionless on the operating table, awake but paralyzed from the neck down by the drugs they had given her. She kept saying, "It feels like I'll never move my legs again." The doctors continued to reassure her that she was fine and that was a normal feeling during a C-section. The doctors and nurses talked casually as they performed the procedure, which, to them, was routine, but to Dani and me was anything but. I get queasy at the sight of blood, so I did my best to keep my eyes locked on Dani's. When the doc lifted the baby up and I heard him cry, my heart lit on fire. The cord had been wrapped around his neck, which is why his heart rate had been dropping, but the sound of his screaming voice gave me confidence that he was okay, that Dani was okay, that I was okay. He spent the next week in the neonatal intensive care unit.

As I write this, our son is six months old. He has already brought me more joy than I ever could have imagined. In less than two weeks it will be the one-year anniversary of losing my brother Dan, and I am as heartbroken today as the day I got the call. It's confounding how our hearts can hold so much sorrow and so much joy at the same time.

I'm heartbroken that my son will never meet his grandpa or his Uncle David and Uncle Dan. But I will do my best to make sure he knows their stories, their legacy. And since Dan loved the name we had chosen we decided to keep it, with one small addition. We named our little dude Cruz Justice Daniel Chitwood.

Acknowledgements

OK, here comes the part where I try not to forget anyone, but I'm certain I will. So let me begin by saying this book is the result of so many people. I want to thank everyone who encouraged me to share my story, proofread earlier manuscripts, and listened to my stories far too many times.

To my friends: Timmy Nelson, for being like a brother to me since first grade. Mark Smith, for years of friendship and inviting me to run my first marathon. Rusty Funk, whose friendship has been a unique blessing in my life. Joe Braik for believing in my dreams, pushing me to pursue them and always having my back. Tommy Fortune, for getting me to countless finish lines. Eric Schoonveld, for checking in on me when I need it most. My pastor, Daniel Hill, for helping me grow in my faith in unexpected ways. And my close friends from each stage of my life—from high school and college, to my years at Youth for Christ, and my friends in Chicago.

There are several key influencers in my life who don't get a ton of attention in the book, but who have shaped my life significantly and without whom there would be no Team World Vision. Some of these incredible mentors include: my high school football coach, Dave Sukup, and my college football coaches Derek Dewitt and Mike Conway. My mentors, Ron Brown, Mike Mantel, Jimmy Mellado, Tim Hoekstra, Steve Spear, and Steve Haas.

I also want to thank my World Vision colleagues who helped start Team World Vision before I even arrived on the scene: Dana

Buck, Karen Kartes, and Laurie Humphries. Amber Johnson who was my first boss at World Vision. Lauren Wilgus, who gave countless hours to Team World Vision in the early years when I was the only Team World Vision staff person and has been serving with me ever since. Kirsten Stearns, who helped lead our team for close to a decade. Marc Valadez, who was my right-hand man as a volunteer in those early years. Katie Hawkins, Michael Baker, and Cam Watson, my managers at World Vision, who have let me continue to dream big dreams. And to my Team World Vision colleagues, past and present, thank you for all you do to invite others into this journey with us. Thanks to Justus Koech from World Vision Kenya, and all of my World Vision colleagues from around the world.

I'd like to thank Rich Stearns and the rest of the senior leadership at World Vision, for believing in me and in Team World Vision, and giving us the opportunity to grow this ministry.

Tim Hoekstra, Mark Wagner, Bethany Jones, and all the others who ran on behalf of World Vision before Team World Vision even existed. Paul JVR, Darren Whitehead, Jon Peacock, Jon Tyson, Bob Bouwer, Keith Stewart, Keith Boyd, Steve Spear, Tim Hoekstra, and Dave Mahar, who were the first pastors to run with Team World Vision and the hundreds of pastors and churches, schools, and other organizations who have joined with Team World Vision — thank you!

The thousands of Team World Vision runners who have stepped through fear to help change lives on the other side of the world — thank you!

My training partners through the years, who have helped me do more than I would have ever dreamed I was capable of — thank you!

Dave Zimmer and the Fleet Feet Chicago family, for your constant support of Team World Vision from the early days until now.

Kristina Olkowski and Dave Louthan, for walking alongside me in the early years as we launched and grew Team World Vision.

I'd like to thank all of the race directors and charity program directors that have partnered with Team World Vision over the years, with a special thanks to Carey Pinkowski, the Executive Race Director at the Chicago Marathon.

Josh Cox, Ryan Hall, Sara Hall, Lopez Lomong, Andy Baldwin, Bart Yasso, Jenny Hadfield, and Alan Webb; Thank you for using your platform to promote Team World Vision.

There are several people who have stepped up huge in making this book happen: Mawi Asgedom, who coached me through the entire publishing process; Marian Liautaud, my editor, who graciously worked with my writing style and helped pull my story together; Michael Forsberg for the cover design, and Victor Kore for the interior design and layout. I could not have done this without them.

Join Team World Vision!

Since 2006, Team World Vision has grown from 100 runners at the Chicago Marathon to thousands of runners, triathletes, cyclists, and adventurers across the country and around the world. People just like you taking on challenges that scare the life out of them while helping bring hope to the poorest children and communities in the world.

Are you ready to step through fear? Are you ready to help change the world? Consider joining Team World Vision and training for a marathon, half marathon, triathlon, cycling event, or other physical challenge and helping bring hope to children and communities around the world. Don't let fear stop you from trying. Close to eighty percent of our team members have never done a marathon before they join our team. We will provide you with a training program that will get you from the couch to the finish line. And your efforts will be worth it as you invite others to support you in raising funds to help children like Maurine.

To learn more visit: TeamWorldVision.org or get inspired at YouTube.com/TeamWorldVision

Sponsor a Child Like Maurine:

Sponsoring Maurine is one of the best investments Dani and I have ever made. Not only have we been able to see her life impacted in significant ways, but our lives have been changed too. Building a relationship with Maurine and her family has deepened our compassion for others and broadened our worldview. I would love to invite you to sponsor a child at www.TeamWorldVision.org/sponsor

The RUNMOTIONAL Project

Over the years Rusty and I have come to believe in the power of everyone's unique story. We just launched an inspirational new project called *runmotional*, www.runmotional.com. We would love for you to check it out, share your story, and be a part of the community.

Connect With Michael

Connect with Michael at www.TheAbilityToEndure.com.

- » Check out pictures of Michael's friends and family from the stories in the book.
- » Watch videos of Michael and Maurine.
- » Inquire about having Michael come speak at your church, race expo, corporate event, or other group/event.
- » Place discounted bulk orders of the book to share with your running club, small group, company, or friends.